LONDON'S
BRIDGES

SHIRE PUBLICATIONS

LONDON'S BRIDGES

PETER MATTHEWS

SHIRE PUBLICATIONS

Published in Great Britain in 2008 by Shire Publications Ltd,
Midland House, West Way, Botley, Oxford OX2 0PH, United Kingdom.
443 Park Avenue South, New York, NY 10016, USA.

E-mail: shire@shirebooks.co.uk   ·   www.shirebooks.co.uk

A CIP catalogue record for this book is available from the British Library.

Shire History no. 1   ·   ISBN-13: 978 0 7478 0679 0.

Peter Matthews has asserted his right under the Copyright, Designs and Patents Act, 1988,
to be identified as the author of this book.

Designed by Ken Vail Graphic Design, Cambridge, UK and typeset in Bembo.
Printed in Malta by Gutenberg Press Ltd.

08 09 10 11 12   10 9 8 7 6 5 4 3 2 1

COVER IMAGE
London from Southwark. Dutch School, seventeenth century. © Museum of London.

PAGE 2 IMAGE
View of the Thames, with the Millennium Bridge framing Southwark Bridge, the Cannon Street Railway Bridge and Tower Bridge.

ACKNOWLEDGEMENTS
Most of the images in this book are the author's photographs or are from the author's collection. The author gratefully acknowledges the following organisations for permission to reproduce the following images:

Bridgeman Art Library, pages 10-11 (Syon House), 109, 113 (Hugh Lane Gallery, Dublin), 144 (British Library); Chiswick Local History Library, page 42; Compton Verney, page 63; Guildhall Art Gallery, City of London, pages 92, 124, 152, 160 and 169; Guildhall Library, City of London, pages 13, 91, 123, 142, 156, 165, 166 and 167; Kingston Local History Library, page 18; London Borough of Richmond upon Thames Local Studies Collection, page 30; Museum of London, cover and pages 6, 7, 12, 25, 29, 33, 35, 36, 38, 45, 49, 54, 56, 65, 71, 78, 85, 93, 100 (bottom), 119, 130, 137, 148, 157, 161 and 168; River & Rowing Museum, Henley, pages 21 and 27; John Rotheroe, pages 41 (top), 47, 86 and 112; Royal Institute of British Architects, page 134; Tate, pages 66, 153; and the Watts Gallery, page 120.

Shire Publications is supporting the Woodland Trust, the UK's leading woodland conservation charity, by funding the dedication of trees.

CONTENTS

INTRODUCTION

IN 1938 an article in *The Times* observed that 'The people of London have a reputation for taking no interest in their bridges'. It is probably still true that most Londoners take them very much for granted and show little interest in the history of the bridges they cross every day on the way to work, about the politics involved in getting permission to build them, and the technical difficulties of erecting them. Although many visitors stop on the central bridges to enjoy the stunning views of London that they offer, probably very few think about the story behind the structure they are standing on.

Until 1750 there was only one bridge in what was then a much smaller London, the next bridge being as far upstream as Kingston-upon-Thames. Today there are thirty-three bridges over the Thames in Greater London, and each one has its own unique story. Twenty are for road traffic, ten are railway bridges and three are for pedestrians only, though all the road bridges and three of the railway crossings also have access for pedestrians. This book is a history of the bridges for the general reader, giving only as much technical detail as is necessary to understand how they were built.

The bridges have been built in many different styles, depending on the specific needs of each location and the technology available at the time. The Thames in

The Thames at Horseferry, painted by Jan Griffier the Elder in the early eighteenth century. The ferry is seen arriving at the north shore carrying a coach and pair. The crossing was not always as calm as this.

London is a tidal river, and this creates particular problems for the building of bridges. There is a difference of about 24 feet between low and high tide; this affects the design of any bridge, as river traffic has to be able to pass under the bridges at all states of the tide. If the gradients were made steeper to create better headroom for ships, there were complaints because horses struggled to pull the carriages and carts up the slope. Another problem is that the riverbed is made up of clay and gravel, not solid rock, so that the foundations need to be set deeply in the riverbed to be stable; this was not always done, especially when the first Westminster Bridge was built.

Most of London's bridges have had to be rebuilt at least once, either because their foundations were damaged by the scouring action of the river, or because a bridge built for horse-drawn traffic was unable to cope with the arrival of the internal combustion engine. The first stone London Bridge, with its twenty small arches, had acted as a weir, slowing down the flow of the river, so that during the coldest winters the river often froze over. When this happened, the river often became the scene of frost fairs, with booths set up on the ice selling food and drink, various sports taking place, and printing presses offering souvenirs of a visit. Even Charles II bought a ticket as proof of his visit. The last frost fair took place in 1814. When the old medieval bridge was replaced by Rennie's new crossing, which had five wider arches, the flow of water increased significantly, so that the river was much less likely to freeze, though the extra force of the water undermined the foundations of several of the other bridges including, ironically, Rennie's own Waterloo Bridge.

The story of the bridges is also the story of London, reflecting its growth and development, as they were built in response to the changing needs of the growing city. It is also the story of engineering technology, from the first medieval bridges of wood to the stronger stone structures of the eighteenth century, the iron and steel structures of the industrial age, and the pre-stressed concrete of modern times.

Anonymous engraving of the 1814 Frost Fair, the last one to take place on the Thames. A printing press sells souvenirs, and two of the bar tents are topically named after the Napoleonic Wars. In the background is Blackfriars Bridge.

With a very few exceptions, London's bridges were speculative ventures, privately financed by subscribers hoping to make a profit from the tolls charged, so that they were built for commercial gain rather than for strategic reasons. It was not until the late nineteenth century that they became the responsibility of a public body and the needs of the community became more important. As a result, more often than not, it was the availability of money that decided the type of bridge built rather than the needs of the local community, and many bridges, such as the old wooden Battersea Bridge, survived long past their usefulness, albeit in a dangerous state.

The oldest bridge-like structure to have been found in London was discovered by archaeologists in 1993 alongside Vauxhall Bridge, where it can still be seen at low tide. It consists of two rows of wooden posts, which would have carried a deck of some sort. It has been dated to about 1550 BC, and it is thought that, rather than a bridge crossing the whole river, it probably gave access to one of the many islands in the river, which may have been used for ritual purposes, such as the burial of the dead.

London owes its existence to the River Thames, and also to the construction of its first bridge. There was no established town here until the Romans arrived in Britain in AD 43. To help create the network of roads necessary to move their troops around their new possession, the Romans needed to be able to cross the river and so they built a bridge at the lowest point possible. The small town they established at the bridgehead later developed into *Londinium*, the capital of *Britannia* and an important trading centre. The bridge was also used as an extension of the city's defences, and the medieval stone bridge had two castle-like towers, as well as a drawbridge, which acted as an extension of the city wall. While London remained a small city the single bridge was adequate for its needs, and the only other means of crossing the Thames in London was by hiring the services of a waterman. This was a skilful job, and a tough one, and watermen had to compete for business at the many river stairs along the banks of the Thames. Outside London, there were many ferries that operated for a fee at all the key crossing points up and down the river, the most famous one being the horse ferry at Lambeth, now commemorated in the street name Horseferry Road. Many of today's bridges were built on the site of the ferry crossings, often by the ferry owners, who saw a bridge as a better investment, though the watermen themselves resisted such improvements as they took away their livelihood.

As London expanded westwards into Covent Garden and beyond, particularly after the devastation of the Great Fire of 1666, there were calls for a new bridge to cater for the growing population, but there were powerful bodies that had a vested interest in protecting their monopolies and preventing it from being built. These were the City of London, which would lose the income from tolls on London Bridge, and the watermen, who would lose trade as the only people authorised to ferry people across the river. In 1671 Parliament debated a proposal for a new bridge between Fulham and Putney, which was rejected because of this short-sightedness. There were allegations that the new bridge would 'destroy London' and that it would so interfere with the course of the river that 'not a ship belonging to us will ever get nearer to London than Woolwich'. There were positive voices too, such as the member who suggested that, when the Thames froze, bridges would allow London to be supplied with its basic needs, and another who pointed out that Paris had several bridges and 'was not ruined'. The opposition won the day this time, but one of the arguments had a certain irony. Mr Boscawen alleged that, if the members approved a bridge at Putney, someone else would suggest building a bridge at Westminster, Hammersmith and many other sites, and that could not be allowed. Unsurprisingly, all the sites he listed now have their own bridge. It took several more attempts to get approval from Parliament for the bridge, which was not built until 1729.

There were similar arguments against the building of Westminster Bridge. When permission was finally granted, the watermen and the Archbishop of Canterbury, who owned the Lambeth horse ferry, were granted compensation for loss of business. Such delaying tactics could not stop the inevitable march of progress and Blackfriars Bridge, which was built by the City of London, opened in 1769. The new bridges opened up land routes to the south and also attracted developers who began to create new suburbs south of the river. Road transport was now on the increase with the improvement in the road system, which was another threat to the watermen's livelihood, and soon new bridges were being built further upstream at Battersea, Richmond and Kew.

The nineteenth century was the most important period of bridge construction in London, as the city continued to expand at an enormous rate, swallowing up the surrounding villages and making them part of the growing urban sprawl. At the beginning of the century three bridges opened within three years, at Vauxhall, Waterloo and Southwark. Vauxhall Bridge was successful in creating a new road connection to Greenwich via Camberwell, with new housing developments being built along the way. Waterloo Bridge, however, was not a great success as it had to compete with two neighbouring free bridges, and Southwark was relatively under-used because of its inadequate approach roads. It was not long before Rennie's new bridge replaced the old and rather dilapidated London Bridge, which had survived long past its effectiveness. Only a few years later, the first suspension bridge was built to connect Hammersmith with Barnes, and Kingston finally replaced its wooden medieval bridge.

In the second half of the century five bridges were replaced, including Westminster and Blackfriars, as the original bridges were proving inadequate to cope with the increasing traffic and were beginning to deteriorate. During this time four new bridges were built, culminating in the opening of Tower Bridge in 1894, which was constructed partly to serve the growing population to the east of the City. This period also saw the arrival of the railways. The first railway bridges in the London area were built at Richmond and Barnes in 1848–9, and in 1859 the construction of the Grosvenor Bridge brought the first trains across the river into central London. The authorities were very reluctant to allow the train operators to encroach on the centre of the city, but the powerful railway lobby could not be resisted for long and in 1864 Brunel's elegant Hungerford pedestrian bridge was replaced by a bridge taking trains into Charing Cross, with Blackfriars Railway Bridge opening in the same year, and in 1866 the Alexandra (Cannon Street) Railway Bridge brought the first commuters right into the heart of the City. As the *Illustrated London News* commented disapprovingly in 1863, '… locomotives are to be allowed to career about and under

OVERLEAF
London seen through an arch of Westminster Bridge 1746–7 by Canaletto. One of the artist's more daring images, with a panorama of London seen through an unfinished arch of the new bridge, complete with a workman's bucket.

The Freeing of the Bridges from toll was a hugely popular move, and people couldn't wait to be the first to cross them, as shown here in an engraving from the Illustrated London News *when Putney Bridge was freed.*

First Man across the Free Bridge — Exciting race

Throwing the Old Gate into the river

the thoroughfares of London pretty much at the discretion of engineers and directors'. There was much criticism of the new railway bridges because, whereas most road bridges were elegant structures designed to enhance the cityscape, the new railway bridges were more functional and cheaply built to save the railway companies money. They were often plain lattice-girder structures, of a type that was soon to be built, mostly by British engineers, all over the world.

For years there had been complaints about the tolls charged on the privately owned bridges, which the general public felt were an infringement of their freedom. Serious discussions about the problem began in the 1850s and in 1877 the Metropolitan Toll Bridges Act became law, allowing the Metropolitan Board of Works (MBW) to buy up the bridges and free them from tolls. The first ceremony, to free Waterloo and Hungerford Bridges, was a low-key affair, but it proved to be so popular that subsequent ceremonies were carried out, with considerable pageantry, by the Prince and Princess of Wales, who were welcomed by throngs of Londoners lining the streets, and many more wanting to be among the first to walk across the emancipated bridges.

Somewhat surprisingly, only two new bridges were built in the twentieth century, at Twickenham and Chiswick as part of the Great Chertsey Road scheme in 1933. It was the age of the internal combustion engine, and many bridges could not cope with the extra volume and weight of traffic and had to be either strengthened or replaced. All three of Rennie's bridges were demolished. Southwark was replaced in 1921, and his masterpiece, Waterloo Bridge, which had started to collapse, was rebuilt during the Second World War. London Bridge, which had been widened in 1902, was finally replaced in the late 1960s by an even wider bridge, though Rennie's bridge was shipped over to the United States to become a tourist attraction.

During the Second World War the bridges were considered to be a target for enemy bombers, and disguised pillboxes were set up by some of the major bridges to defend them. Several temporary bridges were erected in case any of the permanent

ones were destroyed or badly damaged. The Millbank Bridge was located near Tate Britain, and another was built between Westminster Bridge and Hungerford Bridge. Fortunately London's bridges survived virtually unscathed, despite the constant bombardment, and after the war the temporary bridges found a new use spanning rivers in various Commonwealth countries.

At the opening of the twenty-first century two pedestrian bridges were built. Lord Foster's innovative Millennium Bridge between St Paul's and Tate Modern opened in 2000 but it was found to wobble and had to be closed for safety reasons. After many tests and the installation of dampers to stop the movement, it reopened in 2002 and is proving very popular, though it is still called the 'wobbly bridge'. For years there had been discussions about ways of improving the eyesore that was the Hungerford Railway Bridge, and a pair of striking pedestrian footbridges, known as the Golden Jubilee Bridges, were attached to the sides of it, opening in 2003. They too have been hugely successful and offer wonderful views up and down the river.

As for the future, it is unlikely that there will be any more new bridges in central London, but the planning authorities are considering proposals for two new crossings east of Tower Bridge, including one which would form part of the Thames Gateway development, and a bridge for pedestrians and cyclists which can be lifted to allow ships to pass through.

The story of London's bridges is not confined solely to the work of the architects and engineers. It is also about the pilots who have flown under them, the daredevils who have dived off them, and the artists and writers who have been inspired by them. It is also, more sadly, a story of the desperate people who have chosen to end their lives by jumping off them. Most of the bridges have been used for this purpose,

The emergency bridge put up for the duration of the Second World War near Vauxhall Bridge being taken down in 1948.

but Waterloo Bridge, quite unfairly, gained such a reputation, especially in the 1840s, that the newspapers referred to 'Waterloo suicides' and the bridge became known as the 'Bridge of Sighs'.

Many artists have been fascinated by the Thames, and in particular its bridges. The earliest image of London Bridge is in the background of an illuminated text of the poems of Charles d'Orléans, written while he was a prisoner in the Tower. Later, many artists painted or engraved the bridge in detail, and from various angles, and, although not always reliable, these depictions help us to see how the bridge changed during its life of six hundred years. News of the new bridge at Westminster travelled far and wide, and it attracted the Venetian artist Canaletto to London, where he painted the most iconic images of the bridge. English artists, such as Samuel Scott and William Marlow, were inspired by him and painted views of the bridges at Westminster and Blackfriars. In the nineteenth century, Constable painted the opening of Waterloo Bridge, and Turner depicted Westminster Bridge in his dramatic painting of the burning of the Houses of Parliament. Many lesser artists, including Henry Pether and John Atkinson Grimshaw, loved to paint the river by moonlight, with various bridges in the background. The topographical artists George Scharf and Edward William Cooke have left us an invaluable record of the construction of the new London Bridge and the demolition of the old bridge. James McNeill Whistler painted the Thames many times, especially old Battersea Bridge, and he also made drawings of old Waterloo Bridge and the demolition of old Westminster Bridge. His pupil Walter Greaves also painted old Battersea Bridge, but his best-known work is a vivid painting of a dangerously overcrowded Hammersmith Bridge on Boat Race Day. Probably the most famous paintings of Waterloo Bridge are the forty painted by Monet from his balcony at the Savoy Hotel. He was drawn to London by its celebrated fogs, and his depictions of Waterloo Bridge, and the thirty or so pictures of Charing Cross Railway Bridge, are really studies of the changing light and the effects of the fog. Probably the most extraordinary paintings of London bridges are those painted by the Fauvist André Derain, who visited London in 1906. The results are vibrant but unrealistically coloured views of almost all the bridges from Westminster to Tower Bridge.

London has regularly appeared as a backdrop in feature films, and a number of the better-known bridges have appeared in them, usually as a location-setting shot, mostly of either Westminster Bridge or Tower Bridge. As London has become more popular as a location for filming, certain bridges, such as Hammersmith Bridge and the Albert Bridge, have played a more prominent part, but more often than not, they appear fleetingly. At the time of writing, the Millennium Bridge has become one of the most popular London locations for film-makers, including 'Bollywood' directors. Waterloo Bridge is probably the only bridge to have given its name to a film, which was so successful that there are two versions of it.

HAMPTON COURT BRIDGE

Hampton court bridge qualifies as the furthest upstream Thames bridge in Greater London because its northern half is in the London Borough of Richmond-on-Thames, the boundary with Surrey running across the centre of it. The current bridge is the fourth one on the site.

Hampton was a village of minor importance until Thomas Wolsey, who was later to become a cardinal and Lord Chancellor of England, acquired the manor in 1514 and built himself a grand palace there. There are no records of a ferry operating there until 1536, by which time Wolsey had fallen from favour and Henry VIII was making the palace even more magnificent. By the middle of the eighteenth century the ferry was operated by James Clarke, who decided that, with the increase in traffic, it was time to build a bridge, which would be a more financially rewarding enterprise. A Parliamentary Bill was passed in 1750 and work began in 1752. Designed and built by Samuel Stevens and Benjamin Ludgator, the wooden bridge opened on 13 December 1753. It was a decidedly unusual construction, with a picturesque Chinese appearance, not unlike the well-known 'Willow pattern' design. It had seven arches, and there were curious 'pagodas' on each side of the central span. Its obvious charm attracted several artists to draw or paint it, including Canaletto, but people crossing the bridge found the humps made the ride very uncomfortable, and the toll

Anonymous print of the first, Chinese-style, bridge at Hampton Court, probably inspired by a drawing by Canaletto. A drive over the humps of the bridge must have been most uncomfortable.

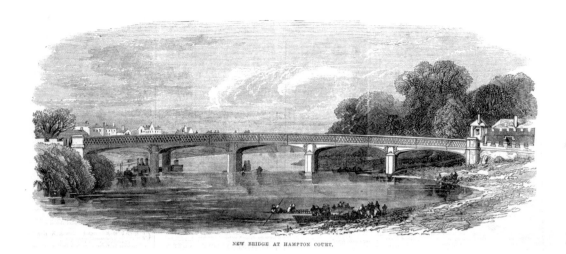

NEW BRIDGE AT HAMPTON COURT.

Engraving of the third, iron, bridge at Hampton Court which opened in 1865.

was higher than for the ferry. It was not a particularly strong construction, needing regular repairs, and it lasted only twenty-five years.

Its replacement, built by a Mr White of Weybridge, was erected on the same alignment and using the same abutments. It was also built of wood but was quite unlike the first bridge, resembling rather the first bridges at Putney and Battersea. It had ten arches, and there was a tollhouse on the Middlesex side. It opened in 1778 and was a financial success, especially when there was a race meeting at nearby Hurst Park. Even though it was a sturdier structure than the first bridge, it was much criticised, as the arches were rather narrow, creating an obstruction for river traffic.

By the 1860s the bridge was owned by Thomas Newland Allen and, to gain public support for his scheme to replace it, he promised to reduce the tolls. During demolition of the old bridge and construction of the new one, a replacement ferry service was provided. The new bridge was designed by a Mr Murray and consisted of five spans made of wrought-iron lattice girders, supported by four pairs of cast-iron columns. To each of the piers was attached Mr Allen's cast-iron coat of arms, and one of these can still be seen on a wall on the Surrey side of the bridge. The walls on the approaches and the tollhouse on the north bank were of brick and white stone to blend in with the palace. The bridge opened on 10 April 1865. Opinions on the new bridge were mixed. According to one critic, it was 'one of the ugliest bridges in England', while the *Illustrated London News* claimed that 'the architectural style is in harmony with the Tudor portion of the palace'. In 1874 the Impressionist artist Sisley lived in the area and painted a number of views, several of them featuring the iron bridge.

In 1876 the bridge was bought from Mr Allen by the Metropolitan Board of Works and freed from tolls. On 8 July there was a grand ceremony, during which the tollgates were taken down and burnt. The iron posts that held the tollgates were later erected outside St Mary's Church in Hampton, apparently to keep grave-robbers out of the graveyard, and they can still be seen there today. The tollhouse has been converted into a bar of the Mitre Hotel, and the castellated brick abutments are still visible on both sides of the river.

In 1901 the London United Tramways Company, as part of its plans to extend its services into west London, wished to run a service over the bridge and offered to pay towards the cost of the widening of the bridge, but nothing came of the idea.

By 1922 the bridge was deemed to be unsafe and a weight limit of 5 tons was imposed. It was clear that the old bridge could no longer cope with the increasing traffic and would have to be replaced. Agreement was reached between the Middlesex and Surrey County Councils in 1927, and the plans were approved by the Thames Conservancy Board in 1929. The new crossing, at 70 feet wide, more than three times the width of the previous one, was designed by Sir Edwin Lutyens and built by the Surrey County engineer, W. P. Robinson. Work began in September 1930 on a new alignment, a little downstream from the earlier bridge, which remained in use until the new one was finished. The Castle Inn, on the Surrey bank, dating from the seventeenth century, was demolished to make way for the new approaches, and the Mole and Ember rivers had to be diverted. The new bridge has three spans of ferro-concrete, which is clad in hand-made red bricks and Portland stone so that it is visually in keeping with Wren's part of Hampton Court Palace. Originally the bridge was to have square pavilions at each corner, in the style of Wren, but, to save money, their construction was postponed and in the end they were never built. The spaces where they would have stood can still be seen. Mounted on the parapet are unusual Art Deco lamp standards.

The bridge was unofficially opened to traffic on 9 April 1933 with a torchlight procession, and the official opening was carried out on 3 July by the Prince of Wales (the future Edward VIII). It was the last of three bridges he opened that day, the others being the new Twickenham and Chiswick bridges. The main ceremony was held at Hampton Court, and it was here that the Prince unveiled a commemorative plaque in the centre of the bridge.

Mr Allen's coat of arms from the iron bridge, now displayed on the south side of the current bridge.

The present Hampton Court Bridge, designed by Sir Edwin Lutyens to blend in with the nearby palace. It was opened by the Prince of Wales in 1933.

KINGSTON BRIDGE

KINGSTON is today a bustling town, proud of its royal connections and a magnet for shoppers. It is an ancient market town and gets its name from the fact that several Saxon kings were crowned here, and the Coronation Stone can still be seen near the Guildhall. The town used to be on an important trading route, and goods were brought to its port from the western counties before being taken downriver. There has been a bridge at Kingston since at least the twelfth century, and the first reference is from 1193, when repairs were made to an existing bridge. For many centuries this was the first bridge upstream of London and, amazingly, the old bridge survived until it was replaced in the nineteenth century.

The medieval bridge had stone abutments and shore piers but was otherwise built of wood, and it was a rather flimsy affair. Over the centuries, owing to erosion and floods, the bridge was constantly being repaired and, on a number of occasions, had to be rebuilt. The Thames was tidal as far as Kingston until Teddington Lock was built in the nineteenth century, and the strength of the tide caused constant damage to the piers of the bridge. The roadway was only 12 feet wide, too narrow to let two carts cross at the same time, and the arches were so narrow that barges found it difficult to navigate through them. Tolls were charged to cross the bridge, and pontage on vessels passing under it, with all the income contributing to the maintenance of the bridge.

Watercolour of the wooden medieval bridge at Kingston by Thomas Rowlandson.

Because of the lack of bridges between Kingston and London, the bridge often proved to be of considerable importance. In 1528 Henry VIII had Kingston Bridge repaired so that his artillery could be transported across it, thus preventing any damage to the more important London Bridge. Later, while he was having his newly acquired palace at Hampton Court enlarged, there was a substantial increase of traffic on the bridge. During Thomas Wyatt's uprising against Mary I, parts of the bridge were taken down to prevent his army from crossing the river, but Wyatt's men made some repairs to it and managed to cross. During the Civil War the bridge was an important crossing point and was fought over by the Parliamentarians and the Royalists, though, except for two brief periods, it was held by the former.

In the late seventeenth century John Aubrey described the bridge in his *Perambulation of Surrey*. He noted that 'In the middle of the bridge are two fair seats for passengers to avoid carts and to sit and enjoy the delightful prospect'. One of the curiosities of the bridge was a ducking stool at the Kingston end of the bridge, used for punishing nagging wives. It was last recorded as being used in 1738.

As traffic increased and the bridge deteriorated, it was recognised that a new bridge was required, and in 1825 Parliament gave permission to Kingston Corporation to build a new stone bridge 100 feet upstream of the old bridge. It was designed by Edward Lapidge, the Surrey county surveyor, and built by William Herbert. The first stone was laid by the Earl of Liverpool, the High Steward of Kingston, on 7 November 1825 and the work took nearly three years. The bridge is 382 feet long and was originally only 25 feet wide. It consists of five elliptical arches of brick, and the façades and balustrades are of Portland stone. Originally a circular tollhouse stood at each end. The bridge was opened in July 1828 by the Duchess of Clarence, who was later to become Queen Adelaide.

The local population were most unhappy at paying what they felt were extortionate tolls, and there were many protests. On 12 March 1870 the bridge was made toll-free, an occasion commemorated by a plaque carved into the stone in one of the alcoves. Celebrations were planned and the Lord Mayor of London accepted an invitation to attend. When, at the last moment, he sent word that he could not come, the Mayor of Kingston went to the Mansion House in person and persuaded him to return with him. There were two days of celebrations, with military bands, a banquet and a firework display. On the second day, a Monday, all the local schoolchildren were given the day off. During the festivities, the tollgates were taken down and burnt on Hampton Green.

Kingston was the first Thames bridge that trams were allowed to cross. Parliamentary approval was granted to London United Tramways to run the service in 1901 and the double track was installed in 1905, with the service starting the following year. Although there was much local support for the service, there were many protests from others that the bridge was too narrow for the trams to operate safely. This proved to be the case, and there were a number of accidents, including one in which a cyclist was killed. In 1909 Basil Mott, the distinguished engineer, was asked to report on the matter, including the cost of widening the existing bridge or replacing it with a new structure. Fortunately for posterity, the county councils of Surrey and Middlesex chose the first option, so as to preserve the architectural

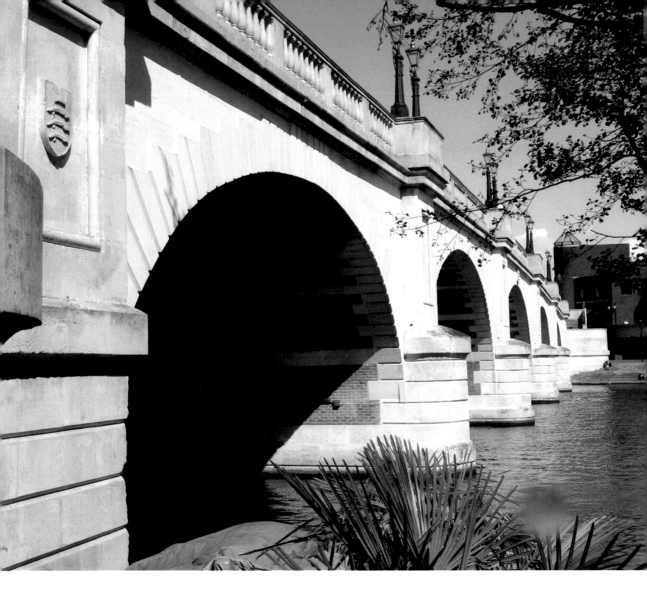

The present Kingston Bridge.

character of the bridge. The cost of the work was estimated at £110,000, of which London United Tramways contributed £10,000. From 1911 to 1914 engineers Mott & Hay carried out the work, adding 30 feet to the upstream side, but keeping the original look of the bridge. There was no ceremony for its reopening because of the outbreak of the First World War. In 2000 the bridge was widened again, adding another 20 feet to allow for a bus lane down the centre of the bridge and cycle lanes on either side of the road, but again the original appearance of the bridge was maintained. It was reopened on 29 June 2001 by the Duke of Kent.

In the 1980s some of the stonework of the medieval bridge was excavated, and the remains can still be seen through a window in the basement of the John Lewis store, by the riverside walk.

Today the bridge is very busy, with a constant flow of traffic, but it is still a very handsome bridge and one Kingstonians are very proud of. It is worth taking a short detour upstream on the Surrey bank to see another historic bridge, the twelfth-century stone Clattern Bridge over the river Hogsmill.

KINGSTON RAILWAY BRIDGE

Because of the local townsfolk's resistance to modern technology, Kingston made a late appearance on the railway map. In 1840 the new line to Southampton bypassed Kingston and went south to Surbiton, which benefited greatly at Kingston's expense. It was more than twenty years before Kingston finally, and reluctantly, gained its railway station. In 1860 an extension to Hampton Wick was approved and for this a railway bridge was built downstream of the road bridge. It was designed by John Edward Errington, who also designed the railway bridge at Richmond, but he died before construction could begin and W. R. Galbraith, his assistant, took over. The contractor was Thomas Brassey, who built a number of bridges for the London & South Western Railway. The bridge opened in July 1863. It consists of five cast-iron spans, which are carried by masonry piers. In 1907 J. W. Jacomb-Hood replaced the

Kingston Railway Bridge in about 1870 in a photograph by Henry Taunt.

Kingston Railway Bridge today. The look of the bridge has not been improved by the addition of heavy service pipes.

ironwork with similar spans made of steel. The resulting bridge is functional rather than elegant, like many of London's other railway bridges, and is somewhat disfigured by the service pipes that now run across it. Today it carries South West Trains' services to Shepperton and Richmond.

TEDDINGTON FOOTBRIDGE

TEDDINGTON LOCK, the largest on the Thames, is now the upper limit of the tidal river. The weir and pound lock were built in 1811, on the recommendation of John Rennie, to improve the navigation on this part of the river. The original pound lock was built of wood, but a new structure was begun by the Corporation of London in 1857, opening on 8 May 1858. It was restored again in 1950. As well as this old lock, there is also the 650-foot barge lock, built in 1904 and used now only at busy times, as well as the narrow skiff lock, sometimes referred to as 'the coffin', which was built at the same time as the pound lock.

Upstream of the lock, and using the lock island as a stepping stone, are two footbridges that link Teddington and Ham, replacing a ferry that used to operate near here. They were built in 1888–9 by G. Pooley, and financed by donations from the general public and local businesses, as well as local government. The bridge on the Middlesex side is a charming suspension bridge, painted in blue, white and gold. Its original steel towers have been encased in concrete. On the Surrey side is a shorter

The girder bridge at Teddington, crossing the navigation channel on the south side of the island.

Teddington has two footbridges. This is the suspension bridge on the north side of the island.

girder bridge, which crosses the navigation channel of the river. The materials for this bridge were re-used from the temporary bridge erected at Hammersmith while the new bridge was being erected there in 1884–7. The crossing is very popular with both pedestrians and cyclists, and the suspension bridge has suffered over the years and at the time of writing is undergoing restoration.

RICHMOND BRIDGE

RICHMOND has long had royal connections. From the twelfth century the manor of Shene belonged to the Crown and over the centuries a village grew up, with houses for the courtiers and others connected to the royal household. After Henry VII rebuilt the house and renamed it Richmond Palace, the area began to prosper. The earliest mention of a ferry at Richmond is from the fifteenth century, though it was probably operating much earlier. It, too, was owned by the Crown and was used by Henry VIII and his daughters, Mary and Elizabeth, who would often stay at Richmond Palace. Two boats operated the ferry, one for passengers and a larger one for horses and carts, but carriages were too heavy for either and had to cross via Kingston Bridge. Further upstream at Ham there was also the Twickenham Ferry, and later its rival, the Hammerton Ferry, which still operates between Ham House and Marble Hill and is the only traditional passenger ferry still operating in Greater London.

During the eighteenth century Richmond and Twickenham became very fashionable, attracting such people as the poet Alexander Pope and the socialite Horace Walpole. It could be dangerous to cross here by the ferry and in bad weather it was often cancelled, which caused increasing problems for a growing population. By the 1770s the lease of the ferry was held by William Windham, who decided that

A watercolour of Richmond Bridge by Thomas Rowlandson, executed some time between 1801 and 1820.

a toll bridge would be a more practical and commercial proposition and sought parliamentary approval for the construction of a wooden bridge on the site of the ferry. There was much local opposition to a wooden bridge, and the chosen site was unpopular too, as the approach from Ferry Hill was very steep. Indeed, a local woman would regularly provide chairs for the elderly and invalids to rest on before tackling the hill! An alternative site was at Water Lane, which would have offered direct access into George Street, Richmond's main street to this day.

After much debate a stone bridge was agreed upon, though the location was still to be on the site of the ferry, owing to the high cost of compensation for the demolition of buildings on the Water Lane approaches. Another problem was that on the Twickenham side the Dowager Duchess of Newcastle would not allow the approach road to pass through her land. In 1773 ninety commissioners, among them the actor David Garrick, Horace Walpole and 'Capability' Brown, were appointed to build the bridge. The 1772 Act of Parliament had a clause stating that anyone causing 'willful or malicious damage' to the bridge would be 'transported to one of His Majesty's Colonies in America for the space of seven years', a rather harsh sentence for an act of vandalism! Another clause stated that any damage caused by boats was to be made good by the boatman.

James Paine and Kenton Couse were commissioned to build the new bridge. Paine is better known as a country-house architect and had worked on the Old Lodge in Richmond Park. The bridge at Richmond was the first and finest of the four he built over the Thames, the others being at Chertsey, Walton and Kew, of which only that at Chertsey still stands. Couse's best-known work is Holy Trinity Church, Clapham Common, but he also worked with Paine on Chertsey Bridge and returned to Richmond to build the workhouse.

The foundation stone was laid in 1774. The bridge is of Portland stone and has five elliptical river arches and, because of the steepness of the roadway, it has always had a distinctive hump in the middle. Originally there were small Palladian tollhouses at each end; there are now recesses where they stood, with seating for weary pedestrians, added in 1868. On the Richmond side was an obelisk giving the distances to Blackfriars, Westminster and London Bridges, as well as more local places; it is still there today, though it was removed for safe keeping during the Second World War. The bridge opened to pedestrians in September 1776 and other traffic was able to use it from January 1777. The bridge was not actually finished, but by now the ferry had ceased to operate. In fact, work on the bridge took so long that there was no official opening ceremony. The bridge was much praised for its simple elegance, and many artists, including Rowlandson, Turner and Constable, were inspired to paint it.

The money to finance the construction of the bridge had been raised by an unusual method, two tontines. This method of raising funds was the invention of an Italian banker, Lorenzo Tonti, who first used it in France in 1653. The shareholders who paid into the fund received dividends only during their lifetime. The shares were non-transferable, so on the death of a shareholder the dividends were shared out among the surviving investors. After the death of the last subscriber in 1859 the bridge became toll-free. Fortunately, there was enough money from investments to

continue with the upkeep of the bridge until 1927, when ownership passed to the counties of Surrey and Middlesex.

By the beginning of the twentieth century the bridge was proving inadequate for the increase in motor traffic, and a 10 mph speed limit was imposed. There were proposals to widen the bridge, but there was much opposition to this on artistic grounds. A decision on improving the bridge was deferred in the 1920s, when plans were put forward to build a new bridge a little way downstream as part of the Chertsey Arterial Road scheme (the future Twickenham Bridge), as the authorities wanted to wait and see what effect it would have on local traffic.

The new bridge opened in 1933, but Richmond Bridge was still unable to cope with the traffic, so in 1934 it was decided to widen it by 11 feet and to strengthen the foundations. Work began in 1937 and, although construction was interrupted by the start of the Second World War, the bridge reopened in 1940. Each stone on the upstream side was removed and numbered, so that when they were replaced the bridge looked much the same as before. However, a number of subtle changes were made to the structure which are at first hard to spot, especially from a distance. The roadway was made more level by lowering it at the centre and raising it at the

Photograph of Richmond Bridge by Henry Taunt, c. 1870.

27

Richmond Bridge. In the stonework under the arches you can see where the bridge was widened in the 1930s.

Richmond end, removing the dip before the hill. In addition, at the Surrey end a new parapet was added above the original balustrade, which is now little more than a frieze against the original stonework. The join between the old and the new sections of the bridge can clearly be seen under the arches.

In 1962 there were plans to replace the old gas lamps with modern fluorescent lighting, but the proposal was turned down as being out of keeping with the character of the bridge, and the lamps were converted to electricity instead. This elegant structure is now the oldest Thames bridge in Greater London, and it must be hoped that it will last for many more years, forming a splendid backdrop to Richmond's lively riverside scene.

RICHMOND RAILWAY BRIDGE

THE first railway line to Richmond opened in 1846, but the London & South Western Railway soon decided to extend it to Staines and Windsor. This entailed building a bridge over the Thames, and the Richmond, Windsor & Staines Railway Bridge, as it was originally called, was the result. It was designed by the company's engineer, Joseph Locke, and the work was carried out by Thomas Brassey. The bridge opened in August 1848 and consisted of three spans of cast iron, and the piers were cased in stone. On the Surrey side the approach is over a viaduct of seven brick arches through Richmond Deer Park.

In 1891 a cast-iron bridge of similar design in Norbury collapsed. The Richmond bridge was therefore replaced by a very similar steel structure in 1908. The engineer, J. W. Jacomb-Hood, used the old piers and abutments, thus retaining the original appearance of the bridge. The new structure is now actually two separate bridges, each carrying one line of track. Further major work was carried out in 1984, when the main girders and decking were replaced.

Richmond Railway Bridge today.

BELOW: *An engraving from the* Illustrated London News *showing the Richmond Railway Bridge soon after its opening.*

29

TWICKENHAM BRIDGE

A NEW bridge at Twickenham was first proposed in 1909, but the First World War and the Depression prevented any action being taken. In the 1920s a new Chertsey Arterial Road was formally proposed, which would involve the construction of two new bridges, at Richmond and Chiswick. The new bridge would allow through traffic to avoid Richmond town centre, which was becoming congested, especially around the old bridge, but it would also cut off the town from the Old Deer Park, and this was the cause of much opposition to its construction.

The engineer for the project was Alfred Dryland, and the bridge was designed by Maxwell Ayrton. Ayrton, who is best known as one of the architects of the original Wembley Stadium, was a pioneer of the architectural use of concrete. Ayrton's original design had two massive towers at each end of the bridge, which, with the equally heavy abutments, looked rather like military fortifications. The design met with considerable local disapproval as being totally inappropriate for the setting, and Ayrton was asked to modify the plans. He first removed the towers on the Surrey side, leaving smaller ones on the Middlesex bank, but he was finally persuaded to remove these as well. There was even controversy over what the bridge would be called. It was originally referred to as the new Richmond Bridge, which was understandably abandoned as being rather confusing, and Richmond Council wanted it to be called

Aerial view of Twickenham Bridge under construction.

30

St Margaret's Bridge, after the name of the area on the Middlesex bank, but finally its current name was agreed upon, as the direction of the bridge is towards Twickenham.

Work on Twickenham Bridge eventually began in 1931, a short distance downstream of the railway bridge. The three river spans are each of 101 feet and the distance between the parapets is 75 feet, with a roadway 45 feet wide and footpaths on either side. The bridge was made of reinforced concrete, the first large bridge in Britain to use this new technology. To allow for flexibility, at each end of the arches are special hinges, which have been made a design feature of the bridge and are emphasised by curious Egyptian Art Deco bronze plates. Also in Art Deco style are the lamps and the balustrade, which continues down the staircases at each end. Some red concrete tiles have been added to the staircase walls to add a dash of colour to the dark grey concrete. At both ends of the bridge is a shore arch over the towpath.

The bridge was opened on 3 July 1933 by the Prince of Wales (the future Edward VIII), the second of the three bridges he opened that day, the others being at Chiswick and Hampton Court.

Between the bridge and the Richmond Railway Bridge are the only visible remains of a foot tunnel under the river, built by the Metropolitan Water Board, probably in the late nineteenth or early twentieth century, though for what purpose is now unclear. On each side of the Thames are curious little circular brick buildings, which were once the entrances to the tunnel.

Twickenham Bridge. Note the Egyptian Art Deco detailing above the piers.

RICHMOND LOCK

RICHMOND LOCK is one of the most attractive Thames crossings in Greater London, its sympathetic design enhanced by its idyllic setting. It is also clearly much loved by the local inhabitants, though their predecessors had to fight a prolonged and hard-fought battle to get it built.

As predicted by Thomas Telford in 1823, the removal of the old medieval London Bridge in 1832 caused huge changes to the tides on the Thames, even as far upstream as Richmond. The tidal flow was further affected by the replacement of the old bridges at Westminster and Blackfriars in the 1860s. At low tide the Thames between Richmond and Teddington was reduced to such a narrow and shallow stream that it could not be navigated, causing some boats to be grounded for up to ten hours. Even worse, the exposed mud became a foul-smelling slime. For many years the local inhabitants petitioned for something to be done, and in 1860 a proposal was put forward for a lock and weir at Isleworth, but the Thames Conservators turned it down, arguing that it would affect the flow of water further downstream. In 1871 the Conservators finally agreed that there was a problem and they commissioned a report, which recommended the dredging of the river. This was duly carried out but made little difference. In 1881 another proposal for a lock and weir was turned down by the Conservators, worried about the effect it would have on riverside interests in the lower reaches of the Thames. They carried out more dredging, but this only made

Richmond Lock from the Surrey side.

matters worse, as the water level dropped even more. To publicise the problem, watermen played a cricket match on the riverbed one afternoon at Richmond!

The residents of Richmond and Twickenham now formed a joint committee to take matters forward and, after a Mr Stoney came up with an acceptable design for a weir, they presented a Bill in Parliament for a lock and weir to be built downstream of the Richmond Railway Bridge. There was much opposition to the scheme in both Houses of Parliament, from the railway companies, a ferry operator and the Dukes of Devonshire and Northumberland, both landowners in the area. Expert witnesses were called for both sides, including the great engineers Sir Benjamin Baker for the Bill and Sir Joseph Bazalgette against it. After much debate the Bill was passed and Royal Assent given in 1890, so that construction was at last able to begin in 1892.

Engraving from the Illustrated London News *celebrating the opening of Richmond Lock.*

Richmond Lock was constructed by James More, the Thames Conservancy engineer, at a cost of £61,000. Its total length is 348 feet and it has five steel spans. The three central arches that house the sluices are each 66 feet wide, and the spans at each end are 50 feet. The arch on the Surrey side houses a 250-foot long barge lock, and there are three slipways for smaller boats under the arch on the Middlesex side. The piers are of concrete and they are faced in Cornish granite below water and Staffordshire blue bricks above. The sluice gates were, at the time of construction, the largest ever made, and are 68 feet wide, 12 feet deep and weigh 32 tons. A clever system of counterbalances was used, which allowed the gates to be raised or dropped by two men in about five minutes. An even more ingenious engineering design means that, when the sluice gates are raised, they turn 90 degrees to a horizontal position and sit underneath the bridge, practically out of sight. This answered local concerns about the raised gates looking unsightly in what was, and still is, an area of considerable natural beauty. Building the lock and weir was a considerable feat of engineering, and it was a great achievement that no one died during its construction.

The lock was officially opened on 19 May 1894 by the Duke and Duchess of York (the future King George V and Queen Mary), accompanied by various members of the royal family and the Lord Mayor of London. Four days later there was a less formal celebration, with a carnival procession, boat races and fireworks.

Two footbridges were included in the superstructure for the public to use, and a toll of one penny was charged, though postmen and soldiers did not have to pay. It was by many years the last bridge on the tideway to charge a toll. The charge was finally abolished in 1938, as collecting it cost more than the revenue earned, especially as people were now able to use the nearby Twickenham Bridge for free.

The steel arches of the footbridges and their parapets are painted in an attractive light green and cream, and there are lamp standards with glass globes at intervals. On the Surrey shore is a brick building looking a little like a railway station, which is the office of the Port of London Authority (PLA), which operates the lock.

The water level from here to Teddington is kept at or above half tide and is maintained by raising the sluice gates from about two hours before high tide until two hours after it. During this time boats can go through two of the three central arches (the first one on the Surrey side is no longer used by river traffic as the harbourmaster's launch is moored there). When the gates are closed, three red warning lights hang from the bridge and boats have to go through the lock, where working boats pay a fee, placed in a bucket let down on a pole. The hand-operated mechanism for lifting and lowering the sluice gates was replaced by electric motors in 1960. The upstream footbridge is now used only by the PLA staff, who operate the sluice gates from it, opening and closing each one individually.

In the early 1990s the PLA carried out a £4 million renovation of the structure, and in 1994 Prince Andrew, Duke of York, unveiled a plaque on the Twickenham side to commemorate its opening by his royal namesake one hundred years earlier.

Richmond Lock. One of the raised sluices resting inside the superstructure.

KEW BRIDGE

A ferry is known to have operated from Brentford to Kew for many centuries, and it is even possible that its origin goes back to the Roman period. In 1659 a second ferry went into service near the site of the present Kew Bridge. It was run by Henry Tunstall and his son Robert and was originally set up to service the family's limekiln business. However, they soon went into competition with the Kew Ferry by accepting passengers, and before long the Tunstall family was operating both ferries.

In 1730 Frederick, Prince of Wales, and his wife, Augusta, made Kew Palace their country home and, as they enjoyed entertaining, the ferry was in greater demand than ever and soon became known as the Royal Ferry. In 1757 Robert Tunstall obtained an Act of Parliament to build a bridge to replace the ferries. The bridge, built by John Barnard, the master carpenter who had worked on Westminster Bridge, had two brick and stone arches on each bank with seven wooden river spans, the central one 50 feet wide. Although not quite finished, the bridge was opened three days before the official opening to allow the Dowager Princess of Wales and her son, the future George III, to use the new bridge. When the bridge opened to the public on 4 June 1759, three thousand people crossed it. As it was the only Thames bridge between Fulham and Kingston, it was to prove extremely

Watercolour of the first, wooden, Kew Bridge, painted by Paul Sandby in 1759.

35

popular, even though the toll for a coach and four was 1s 6d and for pedestrians a halfpenny.

Even before it was built, watermen complained that the wooden bridge would be difficult to navigate, and so it proved. It was regularly damaged by barges, and the cost of repairs was high, making it uneconomical to run. In 1782 Robert Tunstall's son, also called Robert, was granted permission to replace it with a stone bridge. The £16,000 needed to build it was raised through a subscription scheme known as a tontine (a system that is explained in the chapter on Richmond Bridge). The designer of the bridge was James Paine, who had recently built the new bridge at Richmond. Its location was about 100 feet downstream of the wooden bridge, which remained open while the new bridge was being built. It was constructed of Portland and Purbeck stone, had seven arches and had steep approaches, like the bridge at Richmond, but without a hump in the centre. Paine had wanted the bridge to be ornate, with sculpture, triumphal arches and Doric tollbooths, but because of the shortage of funds his design had to be simplified. The bridge was only 18 feet wide, which was to cause problems a century later. The bridge was opened on 22 September 1789, when George III and Queen Charlotte led a procession of coaches over it, but Paine was unable to attend the ceremony through ill health and he died later that year.

The bridge was sold to the Metropolitan Board of Works (MBW) in 1873, when the tolls were finally dropped. The ceremony was attended by the Lord Mayor and Sheriffs of the City, officials from the MBW and many local dignitaries, and the carriages processed to the bridge from Gunnersbury station along streets lined with large crowds. The bridge was decorated with banners and there were triumphal arches at each end. The Lord Mayor declared the bridge open by unlocking the tollgate, which was then carried around Brentford and Kew in procession on a brewer's dray. The day closed with a firework display.

The bridge was later sold to the county councils of Surrey and Middlesex, who decided the bridge was inadequate for the increased traffic levels and would need to be widened or rebuilt. They asked the engineer Sir John Wolfe-Barry, who had recently built Tower Bridge, to report on the state of the bridge and he advised that, because of the need to underpin the piers, it would be cheaper to replace it. In 1898 an Act was passed and Sir John was commissioned to design the new bridge, along with his partner, Cuthbert Brereton, and it was built by Easton Gibb. In 1899 a temporary timber bridge was built and later that year demolition of the old bridge began.

The new bridge is 1,182 feet long, has three elliptical arches and a heavy balustrade, and is built with granite from Cornwall and Aberdeen. The bridge was opened on 20 May 1903 by Edward VII, who was accompanied by Queen Alexandra. A plaque on the downstream balustrade commemorates the occasion, and the inscription on the stone above it records it as having been laid by the King. He did so using a mallet and trowel whose handles were made from wood from the first

This prehistoric flint axe, found during construction of the present bridge, was presented to Edward VII when he opened it. It has been set in a brass mount in the form of the new bridge.

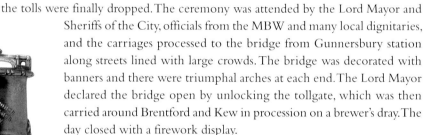

Ogilvy 1899

bridge, as well as a spirit level in the form of the new bridge. The bridge was originally called the King Edward VII Bridge in the King's honour, but the name did not prove popular and it soon reverted to its original name.

At the official opening the King was presented with a number of gifts, including the silver mallet and trowel he had used, as well as a bronze axe, complete with part of its wooden haft, which had been found during the bridge's construction. A beautiful flint axe had also been excavated during work on the bridge and it too was presented to the King, set in a brass mount in the shape of the new bridge. In 1994 all these objects turned up at an auction and were bought by the Museum of London. They had apparently been found in a loft during a house clearance and, although the name of the family was never divulged, it is quite likely to have been passed down in the family of Cuthbert Brereton, the engineer, which suggests that the King had decided not to keep the gifts. Another souvenir of the occasion presented to the King was a chair made from the wooden piles of the first bridge. Photographs show it to have been a fine piece of workmanship, with its three cross-rails carved in the outline of each of the three bridges, but its present whereabouts are unknown.

A view of the second Kew Bridge in 1899 by J. Ogilvy.

Electric lights were installed on the bridge in 1957, when Surrey County Council decided to take down the old triple gas lamps, but local residents protested about the decision, and so the old gas lamps were retained and now alternate with the newer lamp standards.

The current Kew Bridge, the third on the site. The coats of arms of the Counties of Middlesex and Surrey above the piers are a declaration of joint ownership.

OPPOSITE
The second Kew Bridge, painted by James Webb, c. 1880. The water tower of the Grand Junction Waterworks Company, now part of the Kew Bridge Steam Museum, is actually farther away than it appears.

KEW RAILWAY BRIDGE

Kew Railway Bridge looking towards Strand-on-the-Green.

IN 1864 the London & South Western Railway Company was given permission to extend its line from South Acton to Richmond and this bridge at Strand-on-the-Green was built to carry it, opening on 1 January 1869. The bridge was designed by W. R. Galbraith, and it was built by Brassey & Ogilvie. (Galbraith was later to design the Waterloo & City Line, now part of the Underground, which opened in 1898.) It is a fairly standard lattice-girder bridge, with five 115-foot spans, but its decoration is highly unusual. It has cylindrical cast-iron piers, each one decorated with four cast-iron columns with ornamental capitals and, at track level, there is a sort of tabernacle. The abutments are of brick with some fine sculpted stonework, and they each contain a pedestrian tunnel. The bridge was much criticised at the time, and it does loom rather large over the charming riverside enclave of Strand-on-the-Green, but its decorative features make it one of the most attractive railway bridges in London.

When first built, the bridge was painted a rather dull grey, but in 1986 it was repainted in a more pleasing light green. Today it looks a little sad and unloved, as the

Kew Railway Bridge under construction.

brickwork is crumbling, there is a lot of graffiti, and a number of the decorative columns are missing from the piers. The Thames Path on both shores now bypasses the abutments, which have been allowed to fall into disrepair (although the one on the north bank now houses the Strand-on-the-Green Sailing Club).

Today the bridge is used by the North London Line, which takes a meandering semicircular route from Richmond to Stratford, as well as the Richmond branch of the District Line of the Underground.

Kew Railway Bridge – close-up of one of the pavilions.

CHISWICK BRIDGE

THE earliest record of a ferry at Chiswick is from the seventeenth century, though there was probably one in use earlier than this, and it continued to operate until the 1930s, when the bridge was built.

Chiswick Bridge, along with Twickenham Bridge, was built as part of the Great Chertsey Road scheme, which created a major new route from Hammersmith to Chertsey, bypassing, among other places, Kingston and Richmond. The project had first been proposed in 1909, but nothing happened until 1927, after the scheme had been endorsed by the Royal Commission on Cross-River Traffic. The Ministry of Transport decided it was time something was done and offered to pay 75 per cent of the cost, with the Middlesex and Surrey county councils providing the rest of the funding. A Bill went before Parliament in 1927, and the following year it received the Royal Assent, with construction beginning in 1930. The bridge was designed by Sir Herbert Baker, architect of the Bank of England, and built by the engineer

Aerial view of Chiswick Bridge during its construction.

Alfred Dryland, who also worked on Twickenham Bridge. Like Twickenham Bridge, erected at the same time, it was built of reinforced concrete, but Chiswick Bridge was faced with Portland stone, giving it a more traditional appearance. The bridge is 607 feet long and is 70 feet between the parapets, with a 40-foot roadway. It has three river spans, the central one being 150 feet, and there is a shore span at each end over the towpath, which is now part of the Thames Path.

The bridge was the first of three to be opened by the Prince of Wales (the future Edward VIII) on 3 July 1933. Chiswick Bridge was opened at 4.30 p.m., Twickenham Bridge at 5 p.m., and the bridge at Hampton Court at 5.30 p.m.

Chiswick Bridge is best-known as the finishing point of the annual University Boat Race between Oxford and Cambridge, and the marker post of the finish line is visible on the north bank on the downstream side of the bridge.

Chiswick Bridge from the south bank.

BARNES RAILWAY BRIDGE

BARNES was just a small village until the nineteenth century, when great changes were to turn it into a London suburb. First came the opening in 1827 of Hammersmith Bridge, whose southern approach roads run through the area, then the arrival of the railways, with Barnes station opening in 1846.

In 1847 an Act was passed allowing the London & South Western Railway to build a new line from Richmond to Datchet (only a short distance from its real goal, Windsor), as well as a loop line from Barnes to join the Datchet line at Hounslow. Barnes Railway Bridge was built to take the loop line across the Thames. It was designed by Joseph Locke and Thomas Brassey, who both also worked on the Datchet line. To build the loop line, they had to build an embankment so that the bridge had the required clearance of 21 feet at high tide. Some properties on Barnes Terrace had to be demolished for the work to be carried out, but the destruction of one property was delayed until an expectant mother had had her baby. The bridge looked very similar to the Richmond Railway Bridge, with three cast-iron arches, and vertical-ribbed spandrels. The bridge opened on 22 August 1849 without ceremony. At first the line reached only as far as a temporary station at Smallberry Heath, later renamed Isleworth, but from February 1850 it operated services to Hounslow.

Barnes Bridge today, looking in need of a new lick of paint.

44

The bridge was described as 'light and elegant' by the *Illustrated London News*, which also suggested that the new line would prove a great success, especially as it offered 'great convenience to the market gardeners of a cheap and speedy transport for their produce to Covent Garden and other metropolitan markets'. This was indeed to be the case, and the increase in traffic meant that by the 1890s the bridge needed strengthening. It was now realised that cast iron was not a safe material for bridges, so the new bridge by Edward Andrews was to be of wrought iron. So as not to disrupt traffic, the downstream half of Locke's bridge was demolished, allowing trains to continue using the remaining single track. The piers of the old bridge were extended downstream and a separate structure, with wrought-iron bowstring girders, was added, giving the bridge its distinctive if rather top-heavy profile. A footbridge was added on the downstream side, which is still in use today. The new bridge opened in June 1895. The older upstream section of the bridge was never taken down but is no longer used.

In March 1916 Barnes Bridge station opened. It had an attractive little ticket office at street level, built of brick and stone to blend in with the other buildings on the Terrace. The building is still there, but it is no longer used for its original purpose.

The bridge is a major landmark towards the end of the annual Oxford and Cambridge Boat Race, so it is a pity it has been allowed to deteriorate to its present rusty condition. These days the footbridge is closed to pedestrians during the race for safety reasons, but there was a time when the railway company organised special excursions that would stop on the bridge, giving the passengers a grandstand view of the closing stages of the race.

Barnes Bridge on Boat Race Day in 1877.

HAMMERSMITH BRIDGE

L IKE so many of London's bridges, that at Hammersmith was built on the site of an old ferry. In his *Tour through the Whole Island of Great Britain 1724–27* Daniel Defoe said that there was already talk about a bridge being erected here, but nothing came of the idea until 1817, when Ralph Dodd, a minor engineer who had worked with John Rennie, promoted a parliamentary bill to build one on the site. There was the usual opposition from the owners of Putney Bridge, who feared the competition, but the plans collapsed because Henry Hugh Hoare, the banker, refused to sell any of his land at Barn Elms for the approach roads. In 1824, when a new petition was made, Hoare agreed a price and, despite opposition from the owners of the toll bridges at Kew and Putney, the bridge was authorised in an Act of Parliament. The Duke of Sussex, the King's brother, laid the foundation stone on 7 May 1825.

Hammersmith Bridge was the first suspension bridge to be built over the Thames. This was a completely novel type of bridge for carrying vehicles, and its designer, William Tierney Clark, proposed it only four years after the first such bridge in Britain had been built over the Tweed. The design was well received, as it would save money, costing only £50,000. As most of the structure was supported from above, only two piers were required, so that the cost of building multiple masonry arches, along with their foundations, would be avoided.

The first Hammersmith Bridge, in an engraving of 1827 by George Cooke.

The building of the bridge was a considerable engineering achievement, as the river here is nearly 700 feet wide and the central span was to be 422 feet wide. The towers were originally to be quite tapered and were referred to as pyramids, but Clark replaced this idea with monumental Tuscan arches, a motif he was to use again. The roadway was 20 feet wide, which narrowed to 14 feet to go through the arches, and was suspended from four double rows of chains. An eccentricity of the bridge was that the footpath finished at the towers, forcing pedestrians at that point to walk in the main roadway with the vehicles. At each end of the bridge were two octagonal tollhouses, manned by liveried tollkeepers. The tolls were cheaper than at Putney and Kew, and there were exemptions for soldiers on duty, mail coaches and those on royal business, who simply called out 'King' or 'Queen' on their way through, a dispensation regularly abused.

The bridge was officially opened on 8 October 1827, but without the presence of the Dukes of Clarence and Sussex, who had turned down the invitation on hearing that a peer of the realm had already been allowed to cross the bridge. Many other important people, including the Duke of Wellington, were also unable to attend, which was a great disappointment to the organisers. However, there was a celebration of sorts, complete with fireworks, and the bridge was declared open when Lord Ellenborough drove over it.

The new bridge was a great success and Clark was later commissioned to build similar suspension bridges at Marlow, Buckinghamshire, and Budapest, Hungary, both of which are still in daily use. Budapest's famous Chain Bridge, though more than double its length, gives a very good idea of what the original Hammersmith Bridge looked like. When he died in 1852, Clark was buried in St Paul's Church in Hammersmith, and his tomb carries a depiction of Hammersmith Bridge.

Later there was a pier for pleasure steamers connected to the downstream side of the southern pier, with stairs down to it from the footway. It operated from 1843 until 1921, when it was removed, as services did not resume after the First World War.

An engraving from the Illustrated London News, *showing that even carriages and omnibuses crowded onto Hammersmith Bridge during the University Boat Race.*

William Tierney Clark (1783–1852)

Clark was born in Bristol, where he was apprenticed to a local millwright, and he later went to work at the Coalbrookdale ironworks in Shropshire, where he learnt about the uses and properties of cast and wrought iron; this was to prove very useful to him in his later career. In 1808 John Rennie visited the works and was so impressed by Clark's abilities that he offered him a job at his Albion Works in London. In 1811, on Rennie's recommendation, he was offered the post of engineer at the West Middlesex Waterworks, which supplied water to Hammersmith, which was then only a small village. He was to stay with them for the rest of his life, making many improvements.

His new employers allowed him to work for other companies also, and he went on to design the first Hammersmith Bridge, which was the first suspension bridge over the Thames. He designed other bridges as well, including the suspension bridge at Marlow and his most famous construction, the Chain Bridge in Budapest. After a visit to London by a Hungarian delegation, he was invited to design the new bridge, which would be the first permanent bridge between Buda and Pest. As he was busy on other projects, the construction, which lasted ten years, was supervised by Adam Clark, who was not related to him. The Hungarians have always been very proud of the bridge, and both Clarks had streets named after them. Although damaged in the Second World War, it was rebuilt and still stands as a symbol of the city.

The memorial to William Tierney Clark in St Paul's Church, Hammersmith, with a depiction of Hammersmith Bridge.

Clark designed a suspension bridge to cross the Neva in St Petersburg, Russia. It was never built but earned him a medal from the Tsar in 1845. He was also associated with various railway schemes and was consulted on Brunel's Thames Tunnel. He was an early member of the Institution of Civil Engineers and was also a Fellow of the Royal Society. He is not as well known today as many of his contemporaries, but he was very well regarded by his fellow engineers.

He died at his home in Hammersmith and is buried in St Paul's Church there, where his memorial bears not a bust of himself, but a relief of Hammersmith Bridge.

In 1845 the University Boat Race between Oxford and Cambridge was first rowed from Putney to Mortlake, and Hammersmith Bridge became a very popular vantage point, so much so that there were soon serious concerns about the strain this put on the bridge. Up to twelve thousand people would crowd on to the bridge, clambering all over the suspension chains, as well as the roadway, to get a good view! A famous painting from 1862 by Walter Greaves, now in Tate Britain, illustrates the mayhem on the bridge on Boat Race Day. From 1882 the bridge was completely closed during the race, and today the bridge is closed to pedestrians on the day.

In 1880 the bridge was bought by the Metropolitan Board of Works (MBW) for £112,500, and on 26 June the Prince and Princess of Wales freed it from tolls, along with Putney and Wandsworth Bridges. Some strengthening work was carried out on the bridge, but the decision was soon taken to replace it with a wider structure, as it was unable to cope with the increased numbers of vehicles using it. To save money, the

The Prince and Princess of Wales arriving at Hammersmith Bridge to free it from tolls. Note the 'Free for Ever' banner on the tower.

MBW decided to keep the old foundations but replace the superstructure. It was originally proposed that a ferry service would operate during the construction of the new bridge, but after complaints from local interests that this would prove to be inadequate, the MBW applied for powers to build a temporary bridge. This was erected in 1884, and much of it was re-used later in building the Teddington footbridge. The upper part of the bridge was then dismantled, and the pier on the Surrey side was strengthened before work could be started on the new bridge.

The replacement bridge was designed by Sir Joseph Bazalgette, the great engineer best-known for building London's new sewers and the Victoria Embankment. Also a suspension bridge, it is only a few feet wider than Clark's bridge, though much more ornate, with highly decorated towers, with what Nikolaus Pevsner called 'Frenchy pavilion tops and elephantine ornament'. The towers and abutments are made of wrought iron, with cast-iron cladding. The roadway is 29 feet wide, narrowing to 21 feet between the towers, but the footway is cantilevered out from the main structure, allowing pedestrians an uninterrupted crossing.

The Metropolitan Board of Works made sure no one was in any doubt about who was responsible for the bridge. Above each of the tower arches are the date 1887 and the monogram of the MBW, and the monogram is repeated on the capitals of the towers. On the anchorages at each end of the bridge are the royal coat of arms surrounded by the arms of the authorities within the MBW area. Moving clockwise from the City of London crest on the left are the County of Kent (horse), Guildford representing Surrey (castle), the City of Westminster (portcullis), Colchester representing Essex (cross and three crowns), and Middlesex (three swords).

The new bridge was opened in a rather muted ceremony on 18 June 1887 by Prince Albert Victor, Duke of Clarence, who later the same day laid the foundation stone of another Bazalgette bridge, the new Battersea Bridge. The fine iron gas lamps were not installed on the bridge until the following year, and in 1910 they were converted to electricity (the lamps now on the bridge are fibreglass copies). Bazalgette originally had the bridge painted in a shade of pink, but in 1888 it was repainted in bronze green with gold-leaf highlights. After the Second World War it was painted a dull grey, at the time a traditional colour for bridges, but in 1986 it was decorated in its present colours, green and gold. In 1893 two rows of seats were added to the walkways on each side of the bridge, a unique feature among London's bridges, which allows one to rest and admire the view.

In 1902 there were serious proposals to run a tram service over the bridge, which would have entailed replacing it only fifteen years after its last rebuilding, but common sense prevailed and nothing came of the plans. This was just as well, as twenty years later the bridge, now a major entry point into London from the south-west, was becoming badly congested, and in 1927 the Royal Commission on Cross-River Traffic again recommended that the bridge be replaced with a wider one, though, yet again, no action was taken.

The present Hammersmith Bridge.

Unlikely as it may seem, Hammersmith Bridge has been a regular target for terrorists of the Irish Republican Army. The first attempt was on 29 March 1939, when they planted two bombs on the bridge. Maurice Childs was walking over the bridge at one o'clock in the morning when he noticed a car stop in the middle of the bridge, then drive away. He noticed a suitcase lying on the suspension chains, which he threw into the river, where it exploded, causing only superficial damage to the bridge. A second bomb, which went off a few seconds later on the other side of the bridge, damaged the balustrade and some suspension rods and broke windows in nearby houses. Later that morning two Irishmen were arrested on Putney Bridge; they were tried, found guilty and sentenced to a long stretch in prison. The bridge was closed while repairs were carried out, including the installation of a massive brace on the upstream side, which can still be seen today. Childs was awarded the MBE for his bravery. In 1996 the IRA planted two more bombs on the south side of the bridge but, although the detonators went off, the devices failed to explode. A third attempt by the IRA to blow up the bridge in 2000 also failed, but the bridge was closed for five months for repairs.

As the bridge has the lowest clearance of any of London's bridges, it has often been damaged by passing ships. It has also proved unable to bear the weight of modern traffic, and it has been repaired and strengthened on a number of occasions, while its

The Metropolitan Board of Works' colourful coats of arms, which adorn the anchorages at each end of Hammersmith Bridge.

weight limit has been reduced. During the 1950s there were renewed threats to replace it, but the London County Council had other priorities and nothing happened. In 1973 the bridge was strengthened after damage was caused, it was claimed, by heavy vehicles ignoring the 12-ton weight limit. More serious damage was caused in 1984, when four of the suspension rods snapped, and the bridge was closed for five weeks while it was repaired. It reopened with a 3-ton weight limit. In 1997 it was closed for two years to all vehicles except buses while it was further strengthened. Some local residents, especially on the Barnes side, wanted the bridge to be kept permanently closed, but it reopened in November 1999, with a 7.5-ton weight limit, which is still in force. There are now special traffic lights for buses at each end of the bridge, to ensure that only one crosses in each direction at any one time. Despite all the work carried out on it, the bridge still shakes very noticeably when traffic crosses it.

In the centre of the upstream handrail of the bridge is a plaque commemorating the bravery of Charles Campbell Wood, a young Royal Air Force lieutenant who, in 1919, dived into the Thames to save a woman who had tried to commit suicide by jumping off the bridge. The woman made a full recovery, but the officer died later from his injuries.

Beside the path on the north side of the bridge is a metal notice with the London County Council's 1914 Thames bridges bylaws, which lists the penalties for a number of offences against the bridge, such as damaging lamp standards or climbing on it.

General view of
Hammersmith Bridge.

PUTNEY BRIDGE

THERE was probably a ferry from Putney to Fulham at least as early as the thirteenth century. As well as a cross-river service, there was also a long-distance ferry taking people into London, as Putney was an important stage on the way to the capital from the south-west. Crossing the river here by ferry could often be dangerous, especially in bad weather, and in 1633 the boat capsized while transporting some of Archbishop Laud's staff across. The importance of the crossing is also shown by the fact that in November 1642, in the early days of the Civil War, the Earl of Essex built a 'bridge of boats' a little downriver of the present bridge to prevent the Royalist forces getting into London. Small vessels were used as piers to support the pontoons, and there were wooden forts at each end. The structure remained in place until 1648, by which time the King had withdrawn with his troops to Oxford.

By the late seventeenth century London was growing rapidly, and it was felt in some quarters that the capital needed to build more bridges to improve communications. In 1671 and again in 1687 proposals were put forward in Parliament for a bridge to be built at Putney, but there was massive opposition from the vested interests of the watermen and the City of London, and both plans were rejected. Another attempt in 1725 was more successful, and an Act was passed in 1726 for the new bridge to be erected. The Bill was supported by Sir Robert Walpole,

View of old Putney Bridge, showing the iron girder which replaced the three central arches after the bridge was hit by a barge.

the Prime Minister, who, it is said, had once been kept waiting on the Putney shore when on his way from Richmond to Westminster for an important debate, while the ferrymen were enjoying a drink at the inn on the opposite bank.

Commissioners were appointed to carry out the scheme and a number of designs were considered. The final choice was a wooden bridge proposed by Sir Joseph Ackworth, although William Cheseldon, a surgeon from St Thomas' Hospital, was later to have some input into the bridge's design. The construction was contracted out to the King's carpenter, Thomas Phillips. In addition to the construction costs, the owners had to pay compensation to the ferrymen and to the owners of the ferry rights, the Bishop of London, who had his palace at Fulham on the north bank, and the Duchess of Marlborough, who was Lord of the Manor of Wimbledon on the south side. As part of the compensation deal, the Bishop and the Duchess, as well as their staff, were allowed to cross the new bridge without paying. This privilege was often abused by people who shouted 'Bishop' and kept going! The King, however, agreed to pay the toll.

Work on the bridge, to be known as Fulham Bridge, began in March 1729, and it was opened to traffic on 29 November of the same year, although the Prince of Wales had already crossed it a week earlier. The bridge was 786 feet long and 23 feet wide, including a footpath 4 feet wide on the downstream side. It had twenty-six spans of varying widths, from 14 to 32 feet, the large central one being known as Walpole's Lock in honour of the Prime Minister. The piers were protected by triangular structures, which also held refuges for pedestrians. To connect the two High Streets without crossing the river at an angle, which would have been expensive and dangerous, the bridge curved round in front of Putney church. The bridge was financed by a private company, and so tolls had to be charged to recoup the cost of construction and future repairs. There were tollhouses at each end of the bridge, a small brick building on the Putney side, but a much more substantial structure on the

Putney Bridge and Village from Fulham, British School, c. 1750. *Note the large toll-house at the Fulham end, with its bell to call for assistance.*

Fulham side, built over the carriageway like a gatehouse, and which also provided space for the owners to hold their meetings. Each tollhouse had a bell, so that the toll collectors could call each other for help if anyone refused to pay.

With the opening of the new bridge and the improvement in the area's roads, there was a huge increase in road traffic, both private carriages and stagecoach services, bringing in a healthy income in tolls from the beginning. However, the bridge being wooden, much of the revenue was spent on structural repairs, as it was regularly hit by passing river traffic. In 1757 a build-up of ice badly damaged one of the piers, and in 1871 a barge caused so much damage that the three central arches had to be replaced by an iron girder.

One of the saddest events to happen on the bridge was the attempted suicide in 1795 of Mary Wollstonecraft, the early feminist writer and mother of the author of *Frankenstein*. Mary had discovered that her American lover was being unfaithful to her and, realising that they would never be reconciled, decided to end her life by drowning herself in the Thames. She rowed upriver in a boat, first planning to jump off Battersea Bridge, but there were too many people there. By the time she reached Putney it was raining hard. She walked up and down the deserted bridge for about half an hour, so that her clothes would be thoroughly soaked, then jumped off the bridge. She would undoubtedly have drowned if two passing watermen had not seen her jump and pulled her out of the water. Her brief, tragic life was cut short less than two years later, despite a brief but happy marriage to William Godwin, when she died soon after giving birth to the future Mary Shelley.

In 1879 the bridge passed into the hands of the Metropolitan Board of Works, and the following year it was freed from toll in a ceremony performed by the Prince and Princess of Wales. The bridge, however, was not destined to last much longer. It had for many years been quite inadequate for both road and river traffic, and one letter to *The Times* in 1862 about what its writer called 'that wooden zig-zag' pointed out that he knew 'a far more respectable structure erected by savages over a gully in the backwoods of Australia'! In 1863 a new bridge had been discussed in the House of

Etching of Old Putney Bridge by Ned Swain, made in 1884, shortly before its demolition. It hardly seems strong enough to bear the weight of the omnibus seen crossing it.

The Prince and Princess of Wales laying the memorial stone of the present Putney Bridge.

Lords and, in 1880 the MBW decided it was time to take action. They chose a new site, slightly upstream of the old bridge, on the line of an aqueduct built in 1854 by the Chelsea Waterworks Company, whose pipes were to be laid under the surface of the new bridge. This meant that the new bridge, now officially called Putney Bridge, would be directly in line with Putney High Street. The chosen design was by Sir Joseph Bazalgette, chief engineer of the MBW. It was a fairly traditional design, 700 feet long and 44 feet wide, consisting of five segmental arches of concrete faced with Cornish granite, and would cost £250,000 to build. Bazalgette's son, Edward, acted as Assistant Engineer on the project, and they are both commemorated on a stone on the upstream side of the northern abutment.

On a wet and miserable day in July 1884 the Prince of Wales, accompanied by the Princess and their three daughters, laid the foundation stone for the new bridge on the west side of the south abutment, where it can still be seen. The Prince and Princess made their third visit to Putney on 29 May 1886 to open the new bridge, with the old bridge, now a 'picturesque relic', awaiting its imminent demise. There was great interest in both Putney and Fulham, and crowds of people thronged both sides of the river, waiting to cross the new bridge when the ceremony was over.

In January 1909 the first trams crossed the bridge, with tracks down both sides, leaving less room for regular vehicles. By 1914 the bridge was already proving inadequate for the increasing volume of traffic, but the First World War put a stop to proposals to widen it. The proposal was put forward again in 1921, but again nothing happened, but in 1929 the London County Council (LCC) finally agreed to widen the bridge by 30 feet, and the work was carried out from 1931 to 1933. The stonework on the downstream side was removed, the piers and roadway widened and the original stonework replaced, so that the bridge retained its appearance. The old stonework was cleaned to blend in with the new, but the join can clearly be seen on the underside of the arches. The original three-branched gas lamps were replaced and are still among the finest on any of the London bridges. They are of cast iron, and at the base of each one is a reminder that the bridge was built by the MBW, a roundel with the coats of arms of the areas under their jurisdiction. Underneath the two central lamps on both sides are parish boundary plaques, marked 'PP/FP 1886', also preserved in the widening. Because of the widening of the approaches, the two parish churches at each end of the bridge had to lose part of their graveyards, with the LCC having to pay for the reburial of the bodies removed. The widened bridge was opened on 23 August 1933, with no ceremony. By contrast, in 1995, after the bridge was closed for six months for repairs, its reopening was celebrated with a street party and fireworks.

Since 1845 the annual University Boat Race between Oxford and Cambridge has started from Putney Bridge. Looking down from the upstream side of the bridge, one can see the red stone that marks the starting point of the race. At each end of the bridge are churches with very similar towers. Both churches were rebuilt in the nineteenth century, except for their fifteenth-century towers, that of St Mary, Putney, by Edward Lapidge, who designed the present Kingston Bridge. St Mary's was where the 'Putney Debates' took place in 1647, under the chairmanship of Oliver Cromwell, an important event in the development of parliamentary democracy. On the north bank, behind the parish church of All Saints, is Fulham Palace, which was the residence of the Bishops of London until 1975 and is now a museum.

In September 2006 the Thames at Putney Bridge represented the River Ganges for a day. A statue of the Bengali goddess Durga, created for the British Museum by Bengali craftsmen, was submerged in the river close to the bridge as the climax to the Durga Puja festival.

Shortly before Christmas 2007 a number of large holes were discovered in the granite wall of the approach road to the bridge from the Lower Richmond Road. It seems that a local property developer had used a diamond-tipped drill to try to gain access to vaults there which connect to the basement of a property on Putney High Street, as part of plans to open a riverside restaurant. As the bridge is a Grade 2 listed structure, and as no planning permission had been given, the developer was taken to court by Wandsworth Council. It is to be hoped that the unsightly damage can be made good.

One of Putney Bridge's splendidly ornate lamp standards.

Putney Bridge today. Note the fine triple lamp standards.

PUTNEY RAILWAY BRIDGE

Putney Railway Bridge. The two central piers are still protected by their 'starlings'.

WHEN Putney Bridge railway station opened on the north bank of the river in April 1880, it was connected by a footway to a pier for pleasure steamers, but an Act of 1886 gave the London & South Western Railway Company permission to build a bridge across the river to take a new branch line to Wimbledon. It was designed by the LSWR engineer William Jacomb, who had worked as Brunel's assistant on the *Great Eastern*. He died soon after work began in 1887 and construction continued under the supervision of W. R. Galbraith and O. M. Prouse. The first trains crossed it on 3 June 1889. The crossing consists of eight spans of wrought-iron lattice girders, including one land span on the south side and two on the north bank. The abutments are made of brick and Portland stone and the river piers consist of pairs of cast-iron columns. There is a pedestrian footbridge attached to the downstream side.

This Second-World-War pillbox still stands guard over Putney Railway Bridge.

Although originally built for a rail route and owned and maintained by the railway company and its successors, the line was later to become the Wimbledon branch of the District Line of the Underground, which is the only service that now uses the bridge.

During the Second World War defensive pillboxes were erected at the approaches to many of London's bridges. The one that can still be seen just outside Putney Bridge Underground station is a unique survival.

In July 1991 one of the piers was badly damaged when it was hit by Thames Water's *Thames Bubbler*, a 150-foot vessel that pumps oxygen into the river to aerate it to keep fish alive. The bridge was closed for nearly two weeks while temporary repairs were made. The line then reopened, but trains had to cross the bridge at no more than 10 mph. This situation continued for the next six years as British Rail was unable to pay for the necessary repairs. In April 1995 London Underground took over the running of the bridge and spent £9m on repairs, which took two years to complete. As well as work on the main structure, the footbridge was also repaired and a new steel handrail added, though the old handrail was retained to keep the original look of the bridge. To protect the two central pairs of piers, aprons were built round them, looking rather like the 'starlings' on old London Bridge, and they are still in place today.

Oddly, the bridge was never given an official name and it was known locally as 'The Iron Bridge'. Although it is usually now called the Putney Railway Bridge, a plaque put on the bridge to mark its refurbishment in 1995–7 confusingly refers to it as the Fulham Railway Bridge.

WANDSWORTH BRIDGE

T HE story of the two Wandsworth Bridges is not a happy one. Both were delayed in the building, either by financial difficulties or bureaucratic wrangles, and they were both blighted by inadequate approach roads. Also, most people would agree that neither bridge was more than a functional addition to London's riverscape.

The need for a bridge to connect Fulham with Wandsworth was felt for many years, as the nearest crossings, except by boat, were the bridges at Putney and Battersea, which were 2^1/$_2$ miles apart. The Wandsworth Bridge Company obtained permission to build a bridge here with an Act in 1864 and hoped to make a good profit by charging tolls, in the expectation of a new terminus of the Hammersmith & City Railway being built on the north bank, though this never materialised. Financial problems also delayed the construction of the bridge, and there were problems over the design. The original plan was for Rowland Mason Ordish to design a suspension bridge similar to his plan for the Albert Bridge, which had been authorised in the same Act. When the company asked Ordish to design a cheaper bridge, he refused, so Julian Tolmé was asked to design the bridge instead. His bridge was a more basic wrought-iron lattice-girder bridge, which was only 30 feet wide, even though the Metropolitan Board of Works had tried to insist on a width of 40 feet.

The present Wandsworth Bridge.

It had five spans, supported by four pairs of wrought-iron piers filled with concrete, and there was minimal cast-iron decoration above each of the piers. As the *Illustrated London News* commented, 'No attempt has been made to produce architectural effect, the structure being substantial rather than ornamental'. The bridge was opened on 27 September 1873 by Colonel Hogg MP, chairman of the Metropolitan Board of Works.

The bridge was not a financial success, and more money was spent on repairs than was taken in tolls. It never carried the level of traffic hoped for by its owners, partly because of the poorly maintained approach roads, but also because it was not sturdy enough to carry heavy vehicles. In 1880 the bridge was bought by the Metropolitan Board of Works and it was freed from tolls on 26 June of that year by the Prince and Princess of Wales, along with the bridges at Putney and Hammersmith.

The MBW had paid considerably less than the owners had demanded, owing to the poor state of the bridge. In 1891 the board imposed a weight limit of 5 tons, and from 1897 the bridge also carried a 10 mph speed limit. Because of the bridge's narrowness and its inability to carry heavy traffic, it was soon little more than a footbridge, and by 1912 there were demands for it to be replaced. However, nothing happened until the Royal Commission of 1926 recommended its replacement, along with new Putney and Chelsea bridges. The MBW's successor, the London County Council, agreed to finance a new bridge in 1928 but then decided that the widening of the much busier Putney Bridge should have priority. Despite much local pressure, the LCC took no further action at Wandsworth until 1935, when it approved a design by Sir Peirson Frank, the LCC architect. It was to be a three-span steel cantilever bridge, with granite facings to the piers and abutments. It would be 60 feet wide, allowing for two lanes of traffic in each direction, but could be widened later to 80 feet to carry six lanes, though this option has never been taken up. The cost was estimated to be £500,000, with a similar sum being spent on improving the approaches.

The first Wandsworth Bridge, in an engraving from the Illustrated London News.

The temporary footbridge that had been used while Chelsea Bridge was being rebuilt was re-erected alongside the old bridge so that it could be demolished. Work started in 1937 and was expected to take about two years, but construction was delayed by the outbreak of war, which caused a shortage of steel. The bridge was eventually opened on 25 September 1940 by Charles Latham, Leader of the LCC.

Like its predecessor, the bridge is a plain, utilitarian structure, with minimal decoration, apart from the granite pylons at each corner, and painted in two shades of blue. Its low curve was intended to reflect the low riverbanks in the area. Despite the LCC's plans to improve the southern approaches to the bridge, it was not until 1969, under its successor, the Greater London Council, that a new approach road linking the bridge to Tooting was finally opened. The busy roundabout on the south side, where Stanley Kubrick filmed a scene for *A Clockwork Orange*, is one of the results.

This is a rather bleak part of the river, with many industries still operating along its banks, including a cement works alongside the bridge itself. A number of prestigious residential developments have been going up on the Wandsworth side, and their riverside walks now allow public access to the riverbanks, making the bridge more visible than it has been for a long time. In 2007 planning permission was given for a colourful art installation to be added to the bridge, giving it a bit of character. Four 40-foot high cone-shaped glass and bronze sculptures are to be placed on the pylons, where they will change colour with the ebb and flow of the tide.

General view of Wandsworth Bridge, with the Battersea Reach development behind it.

BATTERSEA RAILWAY BRIDGE

BATTERSEA RAILWAY BRIDGE is often referred to as the Cremorne Bridge, after the popular nineteenth-century pleasure gardens in nearby Chelsea. It is one of London's lesser-known crossings, because of its long distance from a major road, and it is little known to rail travellers too, because the rail services using it are infrequent. The bridge was built as part of the West London Extension Railway, a co-operative scheme created to connect rail routes south of the Thames with those on the north side. The West London Railway already ran from Willesden to Addison Road, Kensington, and the new line would continue south, over the river and on to Clapham. Authorisation was granted in 1859 and the bridge opened on 2 March 1863, the same day as Clapham Junction station.

The line was jointly owned by the London & North Western Railway and the Great Western Railway (which each owned a one-third share), as well as the London & South Western Railway and the London, Brighton & South Coast Railway (each with a one-sixth share). The bridge was designed by the engineers of the two major shareholders, William Baker and T. H. Bertram, and it was built by Brassey & Ogilvie. Unusually, it originally carried both standard-gauge tracks and the GWR's broad gauge. The bridge has five river spans of wrought iron, supported by granite piers, and there are six brick arches on each bank.

An early view of Battersea Railway Bridge, painted by an unknown artist in about 1870. The naïve style and unusual subject suggests it may be the work of a local artist, possibly one of the Greaves brothers.

Battersea Railway Bridge is probably London's least-used railway bridge, which no doubt suits the occupants of the colourful houseboats.

The line was never a great success, despite its potential. Although much used for freight services, the public preferred to travel through, rather than round, the centre of London. Troop trains made great use of the line during both world wars, especially after the retreat from Dunkirk, when many thousands of soldiers returning from the Channel ports were carried north by this route. The line was bombed on several occasions, so that passenger services were discontinued in 1940 and did not resume when the war was over. Long-distance services from Manchester to Brighton resumed in 1979, but it was not until the 1990s that local services started up again. Today there are half-hourly services from Clapham Junction to Willesden Junction, where passengers can connect with services to the north, but the through services from Brighton to Watford Junction are under threat. The line was also used by Eurostar trains running between their depot at North Pole Junction and Waterloo International, until services transferred from Waterloo to St Pancras in 2007.

In recent years there have been a number of residential developments along this part of the river, including, on the north side, Chelsea Harbour, with its pyramid-topped tower. Next to it are the chimneys of Lots Road power station, which until 2000 provided the power for the Underground system but it is now earmarked for development. On the south side of the river alongside the bridge is a cluster of colourful houseboats, adding to the area's attractiveness.

BATTERSEA BRIDGE

A HORSE FERRY had operated here since at least the sixteenth century, but the last owner, John, Earl Spencer, decided that more money could be made from a bridge. In 1766 Spencer obtained an Act of Parliament for a stone bridge, but he could not persuade enough people to invest in it, so a wooden one was built instead. It was designed by the young Henry Holland, who was later to become a celebrated country-house architect, and built between 1771 and 1772 by John Phillips, whose uncle, Thomas, had built the bridge at Putney half a century earlier.

In November 1771 the bridge was opened, for pedestrians only, in a grand ceremony. Carriages were unable to pass over it until the following year, after the chalk and gravel surface had been added. The bridge consisted of nineteen narrow spans and it was therefore not easy for boats to pass under it, and there were many accidents during the bridge's existence, including a number of deaths. The roadway was only 24 feet wide, so it was not very practical for those passing over it either. Investors did not make much money from the tolls, as the bridge was constantly being repaired because it was so often rammed by passing barges. Indeed, after the severe winter of 1795, shareholders received no dividend for the next three years. To improve the navigation, four of the openings were turned into two larger ones by inserting iron girders. Battersea Bridge was the first Thames bridge to be lit when oil

Old Battersea Bridge, *a watercolour by Walter Greaves, a Thames boatman who was one of the first pupils of the artist Whistler, who is probably the top-hatted figure crossing the bridge.*

lamps were installed in 1799, and they were replaced by gas lamps in 1824. The wooden fences on either side of the bridge were often breaking and between 1821 and 1824 they were replaced by safer iron railings 4 feet high.

Although the bridge was extremely inconvenient for anyone using it, it was considered to be very picturesque and was painted by many artists, including J. M. W. Turner, John Atkinson Grimshaw, Walter Greaves and, most famously, by the American artist James McNeill Whistler, who made his home in Chelsea for a number of years. He painted this stretch of the river on many occasions, often working from sketches made at night in a boat. His most striking image of the bridge is *Nocturne: Blue and Gold – Old Battersea Bridge*, now in Tate Britain, which depicts it as very much higher than it was in reality. The painting was inspired by the bridge, but Whistler uses its general form to create a Japanese-style picture, quite unlike his earlier, more realistic depictions of it. A statue of Whistler was erected in a small garden on the north side of the bridge in 2005.

The bridge was bought in 1873 by its competitor, the Albert Bridge Company, and its architect, R. M. Ordish, strengthened the foundations with concrete. In 1879 it was bought by the Metropolitan Board of Works, who freed it from toll later the same year. During the previous thirty years there had been many calls for the dilapidated old bridge to be demolished, and an inspection now showed that it was in such a poor state that it would have to be replaced. From 1883 it was reduced to being a footbridge, and in 1885, after a temporary bridge had been built alongside it, it was demolished to make way for a new iron bridge designed by Sir Joseph Bazalgette. In June 1887 Prince Albert Victor, Duke of Clarence, laid the foundation stone in the southern abutment. The new structure consists of five segmental cast-iron arches, supported by granite piers on concrete foundations. The roadway is 24 feet wide, and two footpaths 8 feet wide are cantilevered out from the roadway, giving a total width of 40 feet. The cast-iron parapets are of a rather unusual Moorish design. The bridge was officially opened on 21 July 1890 by Lord Rosebery, Chairman of the London County Council. The old bridge was often referred to as Chelsea Bridge and appears with both names on maps of the period, but the new one was officially called Battersea Bridge.

Despite the narrowness of the bridge, trams operated over it from early on; at first these were horse trams, but from 1911 electric trams were introduced. In 1951 a barge rammed the bridge, causing considerable damage, and the tram tracks were the only thing keeping the bridge intact. No more trams crossed the bridge after this accident.

The bridge's current colour scheme of green and gold dates from a major facelift carried out in 1992–4 (since the mid 1980s it had been a rather drab blue and red). This returned the bridge to its original look, following analysis of paint samples taken by English Heritage. The details of the spandrel decoration stand out most attractively in their gold paint. The original lamp standards on the bridge had been removed during the Second World War and, as part of the renovations, they were replaced with replicas, copied from the only remaining originals at each end of the bridge.

Like its predecessor, the new bridge has caused problems for boats navigating its much wider arches. It has been hit by passing barges on a number of occasions, often

OPPOSITE:

Nocturne: Blue and Gold – Old Battersea Bridge *by James McNeill Whistler, painted around 1872. This famous image is highly stylised and is clearly not a realistic image of the bridge.*

Sir Joseph Bazalgette (1819–91)

Born into a family of French origin, Bazalgette studied engineering with an Irish civil engineer, before setting up as a consulting engineer in Westminster. In 1849 he became assistant surveyor to the second Metropolitan Commission of Sewers, which had been working towards a system of intercepting sewers for London. He later became their engineer, and he kept the post when the commission was replaced by the Metropolitan Board of Works in 1856 and remained their engineer until the Board was replaced by the London County Council in 1889.

Most of London's water supply came straight from the Thames, and much of its sewage went back into it. By the middle of the nineteenth century the river had become a stinking sewer, and there had been numerous cholera epidemics since the 1830s, killing many thousands of people, though the connection between the two was not made for many years. Campaigners such as Edwin Chadwick had called for sweeping changes to be made to the capital's sewage system, and Bazalgette was to bring these plans to fruition. During the hot summer of 1858 the state of the Thames was at its worst, and the so-called 'Great Stink' almost closed Parliament itself. That same year the MBW obtained an Act to start work on the proposed new system of intercepting sewers, which is still in use to this day. The northern section was the more complicated as it involved reclaiming land from the Thames to build an embankment that housed not only the low-level sewer, but also the underground District Railway and a tunnel for water pipes and other utilities. It also provided a new road between the City and Westminster and allowed for the creation of new riverside gardens, which can still be enjoyed today.

In 1877 an Act allowed the MBW to buy all the private London bridges and free them from toll, and it was Bazalgette's job to survey the bridges and put a value on them. Many of them needed maintenance work to be carried out, but Bazalgette also recommended that three of them, Putney, Hammersmith and Battersea, be rebuilt, and he himself

The memorial to Sir Joseph Bazalgette on the Embankment near Hungerford Bridge, a rather modest commemoration of an engineer whose achievements are all still an important part of London's infrastructure today.

designed their replacements. He also put forward plans for Tower Bridge, the Blackwall Tunnel and the Woolwich Free Ferry, though only the last design was carried out. He was also involved in town planning and played a part in the creation of new streets such as Northumberland Avenue and Charing Cross Road.

In 1846 he became a Companion of the Bath and in 1874 he was knighted for his work. He died at his home in Wimbledon, aged seventy-one, and is buried in the local churchyard. Bazalgette was one of the greatest and most prolific of all the Victorian engineers, but his principal legacy is mostly unseen and underground, and his only London monument, on the Embankment beside the Thames at Hungerford Bridge, is not as prominent as it deserves to be.

ILL WHISTLER 1834-1903

This statue of Whistler was erected on the north side of the bridge in 2005.

necessitating the bridge's closure for several months while structural repairs were carried out. One such incident occurred in September 2005, when a barge crashed into the northern arch, causing serious structural damage. While the bridge was closed for repairs, severe congestion was caused as traffic was diverted across other bridges.

In January 2006 the bridge was an excellent vantage point for crowds of spectators who came to see the attempted rescue of a stranded northern bottlenose whale, which had, amazingly, lost its way in the North Sea and swum up the Thames. The whale was transferred to a barge and carried downriver so she could be released into the open sea, but she died on the way. Her skeleton has been preserved at the Natural History Museum, though it is not on display.

The northern approach to the bridge is Beaufort Street, named after Beaufort House, the mansion built here in the sixteenth century by Sir Thomas More. Of that house and its extensive gardens almost nothing remains, but on part of the site, overlooking the bridge, is a splendid recreation of a Tudor palace, built for the multi-millionaire Christopher Moran. At its heart is the great hall of the fifteenth-century Crosby Hall, which used to stand in Bishopsgate in the City until it was moved here in the 1920s. Unfortunately it cannot now be visited. Crosby Hall had once belonged to More, who had his own private chapel in Chelsea Old Church, a short walk eastwards along the Chelsea Embankment.

Battersea Bridge. The photograph was taken in October 2005, shortly after the bridge was hit by a barge and closed to traffic for several weeks.

ALBERT BRIDGE

THE elegant and delicate-looking Albert Bridge is one of London's best-loved bridges, especially at night, when it is lit up like a Christmas tree, but, despite its popularity, it is extremely lucky to have survived into the twenty-first century, as it has been threatened with replacement on more than one occasion.

The Albert Bridge Company was created in the 1860s to build a new bridge linking Chelsea to Battersea, which was a rapidly expanding suburb. There were already two bridges nearby, but it was felt there was still money to be made from charging tolls to cross the river at this point. An Act of 1863 failed, as the owners of the old and dilapidated Battersea Bridge, understandably, opposed the new bridge, as it would take away trade and affect their revenue from tolls. A clause in the successful Act of 1864 forced the Albert Bridge Company to pay £3,000 a year in compensation to the owners of Battersea Bridge when their bridge was complete, thus being financially responsible for two bridges instead of one.

The bridge's designer was Roland Mason Ordish, an engineer who built the Holborn Viaduct, worked on the Crystal Palace and helped design the roofs on St Pancras station and the Royal Albert Hall. The bridge was to be built using the 'rigid chain suspension principle' that he had patented in 1858, using steel rods instead of the conventional chains. Work on the new bridge was delayed until Parliament

Engraving from the Illustrated London News *in 1872, showing the building of the Chelsea Embankment, with the Albert Bridge under construction.*

71

agreed the plans for the new Chelsea Embankment proposed by the Metropolitan Board of Works along the north side of the river, which would affect several aspects of the bridge's design. While these problems were being resolved, Ordish used his new method in building the Franz Joseph Bridge in Prague (which was replaced by a modern bridge in the 1950s). The time limit for building the bridge set out in the Act of Parliament ran out in 1869, but it was extended, and another contractor offered to build the bridge, but still nothing happened. Finally Ordish returned to build it and work began in 1870. It was expected to take just over a year to build and to cost about £70,000. In fact, it cost almost twice as much, and the bridge did not open until the end of 1873, ten years after it was first proposed. It had been planned to hold a joint opening ceremony when the Embankment was finished but, as the owners were keen to start collecting tolls, the bridge opened in August 1873 without ceremony.

The bridge is 710 feet long, with a 400-foot central span, and the roadway is 41 feet wide. The four cast-iron piers that support the towers were the largest ever made at the time, and were cast in Battersea and floated down the river. The 66-foot high towers are made up of a central column surrounded by eight octagonal cylinders and topped with decorative pinnacles. Each pair of towers has decorative cross-bracing to give them more stability. Eight steel rods hanging from each of the towers support the roadway. Unlike the suspension bridges at Hammersmith and Chelsea, the towers are placed outside the parapets so that they do not take up any of the space of the roadway or footpaths. At each end of the bridge were two small tollbooths with a bar between them to stop people crossing without paying. The booths are still there today, and each has a sign reminding soldiers that 'All troops must break step when marching over this bridge', as failing to do so would create the same effect that closed the Millennium Bridge in 2000, causing structural damage to the bridge.

The bridge did not remain in private hands for long. In 1879 the bridge was bought by the Metropolitan Board of Works and on 24 May that year was freed from tolls by the Prince and Princess of Wales. In 1884 Bazalgette, the MBW's chief engineer, carried out an inspection of the bridge and found signs of corrosion; over the next three years the cables were replaced with steel chains, the structure was strengthened and a new timber deck was laid. Despite this, a 5-ton weight limit was imposed, and this allowed the bridge to survive until after the Second World War. In 1957 the London County Council proposed replacing the bridge with a more modern structure, but there was much local resistance to the plans, and many letters of protest were written to *The Times,* including one from the poet John Betjeman. In the face of such opposition, the planners withdrew their scheme, but this only postponed the threat.

In 1964 an experimental traffic scheme was tried, which was to last until 1990. A 'tidal flow' system was put into operation so that during the morning rush hour only northbound traffic used it, with only southbound traffic crossing it during the evening rush hour. By the early 1970s the bridge was again showing signs of weakness, and a 2-ton weight limit was imposed. Some blamed the tidal flow system for encouraging too much traffic to use the bridge. The Greater London Council claimed that the bridge needed urgent strengthening and they were given permission to add two central piers in the middle of the river, though they still insisted the bridge would need to be demolished within fifteen years. Local pressure groups were opposed to this solution, which would seriously affect the look of the bridge. They wanted the bridge to be closed to traffic permanently and to become a pedestrian bridge. In April 1972 the bridge closed for the repairs to be carried out. As well as installing the new concrete piers, the main girder was strengthened and a new lighter deck was laid. In May 1973 a petition with two thousand signatures, including those of John Betjeman, Sybil Thorndike and Laurie Lee, was handed in to the GLC asking them to keep the bridge closed to traffic after the repairs were finished. Although the GLC reopened the bridge in July, it was still their intention to close it permanently, once a minor legal matter had been dealt with. However, a public enquiry in 1974 recommended the bridge stay open, as closing it would cause too much congestion on adjacent bridges.

The tidal flow system was finally abandoned in 1990, mainly to prevent coaches and lorries flouting the 2-ton weight limit. As well as a permanent two-way traffic system being introduced, a traffic island was installed on the south side to prevent large vehicles getting through. By 2006 further restrictions had to be imposed, limiting northbound traffic to one lane instead of two, as many four-wheel-drive vehicles (the so-called 'Chelsea tractors'), which are well over the 2-ton limit,

One of the tollbooths of the Albert Bridge, still bearing a notice to soldiers asking them to break step to avoid damaging the structure.

The Albert Bridge looking its best at dusk as its lights come on.

were using the bridge, and this was the only way to limit the number of vehicles on the bridge at any one time.

The Albert Bridge now seems to be secure for the foreseeable future, and it remains one of London's best-loved bridges. It is reminiscent of a seaside pier, with its lavish cast-iron decoration, its spider's web of cables and the pastel shades of its paintwork. It is most impressive at night, when the lights along the chains are lit up, giving it a fairy-tale look. It is hardly surprising that such an attractive London landmark has made regular appearances in television dramas, advertising and a number of major films, including *Sliding Doors* and *A Clockwork Orange.*

CHELSEA BRIDGE

BY the middle of the nineteenth century Battersea was becoming a busy new suburb and improved communications with Chelsea were becoming essential to its further development. In 1846 an Act was passed to build a new bridge on the site of an ancient ford, and the engineer chosen was Thomas Page, who later built the new bridge at Westminster. Page prepared several designs, including a seven-span stone bridge and a five-arched cast-iron one, but his design for a suspension bridge was the one chosen by the Metropolitan Improvement Commission. Unusually, the cost of construction was to be borne by the Government, and there were debates in Parliament as to whether the Government should own a toll-paying bridge.

Work started on the bridge, which was unofficially referred to as the Victoria Bridge, in 1851. During its construction, workmen found Roman and Celtic weapons, as well as human skulls, and it was thought by some that this might have been where Julius Caesar and his army crossed the Thames. The most important object, found during dredging for the piers, was a superb Iron Age shield, made of bronze and decorated with coloured glass, and now known as the Battersea Shield. One of the finest ever found, it is unlikely to have been used in battle but was most probably thrown into the river as a votive offering. The original is now in the British Museum, and the Museum of London has a replica on display.

The first Chelsea Bridge, in a postcard view from the early twentieth century.

The bridge's general appearance was not unlike the present Hammersmith Bridge. It had four massive cast-iron towers with ornate cross-braces and was topped off with pinnacles. On top of each tower were large lamps that would be lit only when Queen Victoria spent the night in London. At each end of the bridge were two equally ornate octagonal tollbooths. The bridge was 47 feet wide, including a roadway of 32 feet and two footpaths, each 7.5 feet wide. The cost of the construction was about £90,000.

On 31 March 1858, three days before the public were allowed on to the bridge, Queen Victoria, accompanied by two of her daughters, crossed it on her way to open the new Battersea Park. The park had been created by Thomas Cubitt out of the marshy area known as Battersea Fields, and one of the reasons for building the new bridge was to allow access to the park from north of the river. It was much used for this purpose by the residents of Chelsea and Fulham, but they felt aggrieved at having to pay a toll to cross it, and representations were made to Parliament by the local authorities to have it reduced. In particular, it was felt that the working classes, who could not afford to travel further afield, were being denied access to an important new local amenity. Before the end of 1858 Parliament declared the bridge toll-free for pedestrians on Sundays, and in 1875 it was made free on public holidays as well.

Not long after it had opened, doubts were expressed about the safety of the bridge and, on the recommendation of John Hawkshaw and Edwin Clark, the structure was strengthened in 1863 by the addition of an extra chain on each side. In 1877 the bridge became the responsibility of the Metropolitan Board of Works, and it was freed from tolls on 24 May 1879 by the Prince of Wales, on the same day as Lambeth, Vauxhall, Albert and Battersea Bridges.

By the early decades of the twentieth century, the bridge was proving to be inadequate for the increasing amount of traffic using it. In addition, some of the ornamental decoration had started to work loose and some parts had fallen off. Discussions about rebuilding the bridge were held by its new owners, the London County Council, in the early 1930s, and plans were drawn up for a new six-lane bridge. Because of the economic climate, the Government was unable to help fund such an expensive scheme but agreed to underwrite 60 per cent of the cost of a four-lane crossing instead. The scheme would provide much-needed employment at a time when many people were out of work. The final decision to rebuild was taken by the LCC in 1933, and demolition of Page's bridge began in 1935.

The new bridge was designed by G. Topham Forrest, the LCC architect, and E. P. Wheeler, and cost £365,000 to build. It is 64 feet wide, with a main carriageway of 40 feet and two footpaths 12 feet wide, cantilevered out on each side. It is a steel suspension bridge, but with granite piers and abutments. It is, unusually, a self-anchored suspension bridge, a type where extra stress is absorbed by the stiffening girders, which takes some of the pressure off the anchorages at the abutments. This meant that the suspension cables could not be installed until the roadway was in place. The roadway was built in sections and floated into position on barges, and the spring tides were used to facilitate the job of lifting the sections into place.

The design is utilitarian, a reflection of the period in which it was built, and its main decoration consists of the golden galleons and coats of arms on the lamp standards at each end of the bridge. The LCC crest takes pride of place on the outside of the posts on both sides of the bridge. On the inner sides are the crests of the three old Metropolitan Boroughs served by the bridge. On the south side is that of Battersea, with the dove of peace. On the north side are the coats of arms of Chelsea and Westminster, the former with the winged bull, lion, boar and stag, all in splendid gold on a red background, the latter with a portcullis and Tudor roses. Note the unusual design of the lamps on the main part of the bridge, which have been cleverly integrated into the main structure.

The bridge was finished five months ahead of schedule and was opened on 6 May 1937 by the Prime Minister of Canada, W. L. Mackenzie King, who was in London for the Coronation of George VI. He may also have been invited because the roadway was lined with Douglas fir from British Columbia.

From the 1950s the bridge became a meeting place for motorcyclists every Friday night, when they would put their motorcycles through their paces and race each other across the bridge into the early hours of the morning. In 1970 there was a confrontation on the bridge between two rival gangs, in which a 'Hell's Angel' was shot with a sawn-off shotgun. 'Bikers' continue to meet on the bridge and carry out their stunts as before, but their activities are now somewhat curtailed, after complaints about the noise from residents in the new luxury flats overlooking the bridge.

The bridge has been redecorated in a rather elegant red and white colour scheme, with the balustrades a fetching purple. The whole structure is attractively illuminated at night, with fairy lights along the towers and suspension chains, and dramatically floodlit from below, complementing the neighbouring Albert Bridge.

Chelsea Bridge in 2007, soon after it received a fresh coat of paint.

GROSVENOR RAILWAY BRIDGE

T HE Grosvenor Railway Bridge, which is also known as the Victoria Bridge, was
the first railway bridge to be built over the Thames in central London. In July
1858 authorisation was given for a new railway line to be built from Battersea to a
new terminus at Victoria Street, passing along the bed of the disused Grosvenor
Canal (which gave its name to the bridge). The bridge was designed by John Fowler
for the London, Brighton & South Coast Railway and consisted of five wrought-iron
spans carrying two tracks of mixed gauge; this allowed the line to be used by the
Great Western Railway, which was the only company to use the broad gauge. Work
started on 9 June 1859 and the bridge opened exactly a year later.

A few years later the London, Chatham & Dover Railway also got permission to
operate into Victoria station and proposed to build its own bridge over the river. As
traffic had been growing and the LB&SCR needed more lines, the two companies
agreed to work together to build a second bridge alongside the old one on the
downstream side. This was built by Sir Charles Fox to match the first one, and opened
in December 1866. It added five tracks, making the structure the widest railway
bridge anywhere in the world. Before it opened, eight of the heaviest locomotives
were driven over the bridge to test the strength of the structure.

Image from the
Illustrated London
News *showing the*
construction of the
Grosvenor Railway
Bridge.

By the end of the century even this bridge could not cope with the demand, so in 1907 a third bridge was added. The whole thing was now 178 feet wide and carried ten lines of track. Between 1963 and 1967 the bridge was completely modernised, when the whole superstructure was replaced and the piers were strengthened. A new method of construction was used, in which each 50-ton section was assembled off-site and floated into position on barges. During the building work at least seven tracks were kept open, so that services were not interrupted. The end result is, in fact, ten separate single-track bridges.

Rail travellers on their way into Victoria cannot fail to see, sitting sadly alongside the track to the south of the bridge, the empty shell of Battersea Power Station. It closed in 1982 and there have been several unsuccessful plans to turn it into a leisure complex, which would involve a dedicated rail service over the bridge from Victoria. Planning permission has been granted, but in 2006 the site was sold to new owners, who have put forward new proposals.

Grosvenor Railway Bridge with the empty shell of the Battersea Power Station in the background.

VAUXHALL BRIDGE

IN the early thirteenth century Falkes de Breauté, a mercenary from Gascony and
friend of King John, built himself a manor house close to the river near the present
MI6 building. Known as Fulkes' Hall, it gave its name to the area now known as
Vauxhall, which in turn gave its name to a famous pleasure garden, the Russian word
for a railway station and, of course, a bridge.

   The first Vauxhall Bridge was the first cast-iron bridge to be built over the
Thames. It was also, unusually, built as part of a town-planning scheme, rather than
in response to growing congestion in the area. By constructing a new route from
Hyde Park Corner through Kennington and on to Greenwich, it was hoped to
open up the south side of the river to development. At the time there was little
there but the famous Vauxhall Pleasure Gardens, which had been operating since the
seventeenth century.

   An Act was passed in 1809 authorising the building of the bridge, but the scheme
was under-financed and went through three architects before it was finally built.
John Rennie was originally commissioned to build a stone bridge of seven arches,
and the foundation stone of the Middlesex abutment was laid on 9 May 1811 by
Lord Dundas, representing the Prince Regent, after whom the bridge was to be
named. Money was soon a problem and the company decided to build a cheaper

*The first Vauxhall Bridge
in an engraving by
I. C. Varrall, published in
the guidebook* Walks
Through London *in
1817. The massive
building on the right is
the Millbank
Penitentiary, which was
demolished in 1903. Tate
Britain now occupies the
site.*

iron bridge instead, and so Rennie designed a bridge of eleven spans that could be built for half the price of the stone bridge. Surprisingly, the company rejected his design and asked J. Grellier to build one of nine arches to the design of Samuel Bentham, the brother of the philosopher Jeremy Bentham. However, the Thames Conservators were not happy about the way the piers were being constructed and had the work inspected by James Walker, one of the most important civil engineers of the time. The second scheme was also abandoned and Walker was now invited to build a bridge of nine cast-iron arches with stone piers. The bridge finally opened on 4 June 1816 as the Regent Bridge, though its name was soon changed to Vauxhall Bridge.

The receipts from tolls were not always as great as had been hoped and, after the cost of repairs was taken into account, the dividend paid to the shareholders was often quite low. Income increased considerably after 1838, when Nine Elms station was made the terminus of the London & South Western Railway, but fell away again after the station was closed when a line via Vauxhall took services to the new terminus at Waterloo station, which opened in 1848. (A Russian delegation was so impressed by the new Vauxhall station that the word *voksal* entered the Russian language as the word for railway station.)

Takings were also high on days when Vauxhall Gardens put on their popular balloon ascents, as crowds thronged the neighbouring streets, as well as the bridge itself, to witness the fearless 'aeronauts' (as *The Times* called them) taking to the air. (In the 1990s a tethered balloon operated from Spring Gardens, on the site of Vauxhall Gardens, offering panoramic views over London, but it closed in 2001, unable to compete with the London Eye.) Vauxhall Bridge was a good viewpoint for a rather more bizarre kind of entertainment in September 1844, when spectators could witness Mr Barry, a clown from Astley's Theatre, sail from there to Westminster Bridge in a washtub pulled by a pair of geese.

In 1879 the bridge was bought by the Metropolitan Board of Works for £255,000 and freed from toll. In 1881 the two central piers were found to be unstable as a result of scouring by the Thames, and they were removed, creating a larger central arch. However, the bridge was soon found to be in a poor state and, despite further work to strengthen the foundations, there were calls for it to be replaced. In 1895 the London County Council, the bridge's new owners, obtained permission from Parliament to build a new bridge, and in 1898 demolition of the old bridge started and a temporary bridge was put up. There were to be many delays in the construction of the new bridge, beginning with the vociferous criticism from many quarters of the first design for a steel bridge by the LCC's resident engineer, Sir Alexander Binnie. The LCC's response was to ask him to design a bridge of granite-clad concrete, which was greeted with less condemnation than his first design, but was still not popular in architectural circles. Work on the foundations was started but, during the construction, it was found that the clay would not be able to take the weight of a concrete and granite bridge, so, with the piers already built, it was now decided that the superstructure would be built of steel instead. Although Binnie was due to retire from the LCC, he worked with his replacement, Maurice Fitzmaurice, on the new design. Finally, five years later than originally planned, the bridge was opened by the

Vauxhall Bridge, with its distinctive statues. Behind is Terry Farrell's Vauxhall Cross building, which houses MI6.

Prince of Wales (the future George V) on 26 May 1906. Its construction had cost £437,000 and taken eleven years.

The bridge is 80 feet wide and 809 feet long and consists of five steel arches supported by granite piers. When it opened it was fairly plain, with little decoration, and many influential architects had complained that the LCC had not consulted any architects in the design of the bridge. To counter such criticism, in 1903 the council had asked its own architect, W. E. Riley, to look into possible decorative elements, and he suggested adding sculptural groups on the cutwaters and two 60-foot pylons topped by statues at the Westminster end of the bridge. The idea of the pylons was eventually dropped for financial reasons, but, after consultation with the architect Richard Norman Shaw, it was decided instead to erect monumental bronze statues above each of the piers. Alfred Drury was selected as the principal sculptor, to be assisted by George Frampton and Frederick Pomeroy, but Frampton dropped out through pressures of work and the sculpture was carried out jointly by Drury and

Pomeroy. Each of the monumental statues weighs about 2 tons, and they were installed in the autumn of 1907. Looking downstream are Drury's representations of *Science* (holding a globe), the *Fine Arts*, *Local Government* and *Education*. On the upstream side are Pomeroy's figures of *Pottery*, *Engineering* (holding a steam engine), *Architecture* (with a model of St Paul's Cathedral) and *Agriculture*. Vauxhall Bridge is still the only one of London's Thames bridges to be decorated with sculpture.

The bridge originally had rather basic 8-foot high iron railings, but in 1973 they were replaced by the Greater London Council with the present, much lower balustrade, which, though more attractive than the original, was strongly criticised as an act of vandalism in some quarters.

The new Vauxhall Bridge was the first bridge in central London to carry trams. At first, it was crossed by the old-fashioned horse-drawn trams, but they soon gave way to the new electric trams. The last ones ran in 1951, when they were replaced in turn by buses. Another 'first' for the bridge came in 1968, when, along with Park Lane, it became the first street in London to have a bus lane. During the weekday evening rush hours, the central lane was reserved for southbound buses only.

Traffic over the bridge soon increased considerably and Vauxhall Cross, at the Lambeth end of the bridge, became seriously congested. In the 1930s a new traffic system was created, which included a huge 'roundabout', forcing vehicles going from Kennington towards the bridge to take a long detour. In the 1960s the Greater London Council proposed further changes, including a massive flyover, but these were turned down by Parliament. Vauxhall Cross was completely reconfigured in 2004, with a new bus station at its centre, topped by a striking ski-jump roof, the work of Arup Associates.

Since the late 1970s there have been a number of controversial schemes to erect skyscrapers on unoccupied sites alongside the bridge on the south bank. The first was the infamous 'Green Giant', which was planned for a site opposite the Tate, but this was rejected in 1980 as being too overpowering for the area. A competition was later held for a development on both sides of the bridge, but the winning developer was unable to raise the money to build it, and the site remained undeveloped for many years. The downstream side is now occupied by the Vauxhall Cross building designed by Terry Farrell, which was completed in 1995. It houses MI6, the secret service, and everything has been designed so that one cannot see what is going on inside. On the upstream side are the towers of the St George Wharf residential development, with its unusual gull-wing roofs, which opened in 2006.

Looking downstream from the bridge, there are good views down to Lambeth Bridge and beyond to the London Eye. Over to the left is Tate Britain, the Pimlico branch of the Tate, which houses the British collections. A very striking vessel to be seen here occasionally is a bright yellow Second World War DUKW amphibious craft, which drives down a slipway on the right into the Thames as part an unusual sightseeing tour of the capital.

Upstream from the bridge on the south side is an outfall pipe with water pouring from it. This is where the now enclosed River Effra reaches the Thames. Very close to here, and visible only at low tide, are the timbers of a Bronze Age causeway discovered in 1993 (see page 8).

OVERLEAF:
Frederick Pomeroy's monumental bronze statue, Agriculture, *on the upstream side of Vauxhall Bridge.*

LAMBETH BRIDGE

LAMBETH BRIDGE was built on the site of a horse ferry owned by the Archbishops of Canterbury, whose London home was Lambeth Palace, situated on the banks of the Thames almost opposite the Palace of Westminster. The ferry had operated under licence since at least the early sixteenth century and was one of the few places on the river where one could cross with a coach and horses. It was not always a safe crossing, and Archbishop Laud lost most of his possessions when the ferry sank in 1633 while he was moving into the palace. Both James I and Oliver Cromwell ended up in the Thames when the ferry and their coaches sank.

Understandably, neither the Archbishop nor the watermen operating the service were happy about the proposal for a new bridge at Westminster and they fought for substantial compensation; soon after the bridge opened in 1750 the horse ferry service closed, though a passenger ferry continued for a while longer. The ferry is today commemorated in the street name Horseferry Road.

By the beginning of the nineteenth century Lambeth was beginning to develop and there were a number of attempts to build a bridge on the site of the old ferry, but they all failed, either because they were rejected by Parliament or because the developers could not raise the necessary funds. One of the oddest proposals, from Thomas Motley in 1845, was for a two-tier iron bridge, with shops on the upper level.

A. E. Pearce's watercolour Millbank *from 1912, which shows the first Lambeth Bridge. It comes as a surprise to realise how industrial the north bank still was at this date.*

In 1854 a Select Committee recommended the construction of four new bridges over the Thames, including one here, and an Act was passed in 1861 for a suspension bridge at Lambeth. It was designed by Peter William Barlow, who had already had a successful career as a railway engineer but had recently become interested in the design of bridges. His most important contribution to civil engineering was the development of a tunnel shield, with which he built the short-lived Tower Subway. The shield, with modifications, was later to be used to build the deep-level Underground lines.

Barlow's suspension bridge had three equal spans and was built using some of his new techniques. Above the abutments at each end of the bridge were a pair of braced towers, and above the cylindrical cast-iron piers were two more pairs of towers. Between them stretched the suspension chains and, to withstand the strongest gale, the chains were stiffened with vertical and diagonal ties, creating a lattice effect. Unusually, the cables were attached to the towers, making the structure more rigid than with the more traditional method, where the cables passed over rollers. To prevent lateral movement, under the main decking he added two longitudinal box girders, with wrought-iron cross-girders laid at 4-foot intervals. The bridge was 32 feet wide, with a 20-foot roadway and two footpaths 6 feet wide. The footpaths were cantilevered out on each side on iron brackets, their paving made of Portland stone from old Westminster Bridge, which was currently being rebuilt.

The Prince of Wales freeing Lambeth Bridge from tolls in 1879.

The bridge opened on 10 November 1862, the birthday of the Prince of Wales, and for the first week it was toll-free. The bridge's construction had cost less than £50,000, so it was expected to be a financial success, but it was not universally admired. Dickens called it 'on the whole, the ugliest ever built', and *The Times* admitted that 'it was not a handsome structure'. Unfortunately there were also rumours going around that the bridge was unsafe and many people refused to use it. The toll revenue was therefore well below expectations, and much of it came from pedestrians. The Metropolitan Board of Works bought the bridge in 1879 for £36,000, though the bridge company had demanded £100,000. On 24 May 1879 it was freed from tolls by the Prince and Princess of Wales, along with four other bridges, in a popular act which saw the streets thronged with spectators.

Unfortunately, as Barlow was an inexperienced bridge-builder, and as he had been forced to build the bridge on the cheap, it was not long before serious problems became apparent. Within ten years of its freeing, it was clear that the bridge was in a poor state, with badly corroded ironwork, because it had not received any anti-rust treatment when it was installed. In 1887 Sir Benjamin Baker, the engineer of the Forth Railway Bridge, inspected the bridge and found that the anchorages in the abutments were failing, and repairs were carried out. By now it was clear that the bridge was unable to cope with the extra traffic and needed replacing, but the London County Council, which now owned the bridge, decided that the replacement of Vauxhall Bridge had to take priority. By 1900 gates had been installed at each end of the bridge so that it could be closed if it became too crowded. In 1905 the LCC had to impose a 2.5-ton weight limit on the bridge, and traffic was forced to cross it at a walking pace. In 1910 they banned all vehicular traffic from using the bridge, so that it became a footbridge for the last years of its life, and the gates were often closed if it was felt the bridge was getting too crowded.

Proposals for a new bridge were discussed for years by the LCC, but money was not available for such an undertaking. In 1912 and 1913 they made applications to Parliament for permission to rebuild it, but they were rejected, as it was felt that the design was unsympathetic to that of the Palace of Westminster, and even the Archbishop of Canterbury came out against it. Then the war intervened, and not until the 1920s was a new bridge seriously considered again, though by now it was needed to take pressure off Westminster and Vauxhall Bridges, which were becoming more and more congested. Parliamentary approval was granted in 1924, though nothing happened for a few years, while discussions continued over the design proposed for such a sensitive site. The project also got caught up in the wider discussions about river crossings in London, which led to the report of the Royal Commission on Cross-River Traffic in 1926. In some quarters there were people who questioned the need for the bridge at all, and Lord Lee of Fareham, the chairman of the Commission, said that it 'started from nowhere, went nowhere, and did not contribute in the slightest degree to a solution of any item of the traffic problem'.

In 1927 work began on improving the approaches on both sides of the river, including the removal of some old wharves on the Westminster shore. The southern approach was to be about 80 feet further upstream, so that the new bridge did not pass too close to Lambeth Palace. In 1929 a temporary footbridge was built and in June work on the demolition of Barlow's bridge at last began. The new bridge was designed by Sir George Humphreys, the LCC engineer, with G. Topham Forrest and Sir Reginald Blomfield acting as architectural consultants. The original estimate for the scheme had been £638,000, but the final cost, including the approaches, was nearly £1 million.

The bridge is of five segmental steel arches, and the piers and abutments are clad in Cornish granite. The central span is 165 feet wide, the next two 149 feet, and the shore spans are 125 feet. The bridge is 60 feet wide, with a roadway of 36 feet and two footpaths 12 feet wide. The balustrade is of cast iron, and sitting on it between the piers are two unusual cast-iron lattice-work lamps. Above each pier are the carved LCC coats of arms, flanked by dolphins, and above them are Art Deco lamp standards in the form of obelisks, mirroring the pairs of larger obelisks at each end of the bridge. These four obelisks are the most prominent element of the bridge; they are topped with what are often referred to as pineapples and are said to commemorate the Tradescants, the royal gardeners who lived in Lambeth and are said to have introduced the pineapple to Britain. When the bridge was opened, these 'pineapples' became the subject of much debate, and the local newspaper, the *South London Press*, made some enquiries. Neither of the bridge's architects would comment, but Topham Forrest's secretary said: 'So far as is known they are just decorations. I don't know if the form is traditional, but it is certainly not original.' The 'pineapples' look much more like pine cones, which have been used since ancient times as a decorative motif but are also a symbol of welcome or good luck.

The temporary bridge was taken down in May 1932, and pedestrians were allowed to use one of the footpaths before the bridge was officially opened by George V, accompanied by Queen Mary, on 19 July. A pavilion for more than a thousand guests was set up on the new roundabout at the Westminster end of the bridge, and other guests were entertained on boats moored alongside the bridge. After the usual speeches, the King opened the bridge by pushing a switch that opened the temporary barriers. The King and Queen then drove across the bridge, which was lined on both sides by schoolchildren from both Lambeth and Westminster. Huge crowds had come to watch the opening and after the ceremony the bridge was filled with people wanting to be among the first to cross it.

Rather like Southwark Bridge, Lambeth Bridge has never been one of London's busiest, as it is not on a major through route. Trams never crossed it, and the tramline crossing its southern end was seen by some as an impediment to vehicular traffic. The present roundabout on the Lambeth side was not created until the 1940s.

Lambeth Bridge today, with the towers of Westminster Abbey and the Victoria Tower of the Houses of Parliament in the background.

The bridge is painted mostly in red, which is the colour of the seats in the House of Lords, whose chamber is at this end of the Houses of Parliament. Similarly, the predominant colour on Westminster Bridge is green, the colour of the seating in the House of Commons. Lambeth Bridge offers one of the finest views of the Houses of Parliament and Westminster Bridge, with the medieval gatehouse of Lambeth Palace on the right. Looking upstream, the view is more modern, with the glass Millbank Tower on the right and a huddle of contemporary buildings at the southern end of Vauxhall Bridge. On the north bank, on the left-hand corner of Horseferry Road, is Thames House, built at the same time as the bridge, which now houses MI5, the country's domestic secret service organisation.

The obelisks on the south side of Lambeth Bridge, crowned by golden pine cones.

WESTMINSTER BRIDGE

T ODAY it seems extraordinary that London had to wait until the middle of the eighteenth century for a second bridge over the Thames, even though the city had by then spread westwards well beyond its old medieval boundaries. Indeed, until Putney Bridge was opened in 1729 there was no bridge between London Bridge and Kingston. This was due to the combination of the vested interests of the City, which received the lucrative toll revenue from London Bridge, and the watermen, who had a monopoly on boat services across as well as up and down the Thames. The Archbishop of Canterbury added his own protest, as he owned the rights to the Lambeth horse ferry, which brought in considerable income over the years.

During the seventeenth century various attempts had been made to build a new bridge close to the horse ferry and, in 1664, discussions were held on the subject at the Privy Council. Although the representative of the City of Westminster was in favour, as the bridge would offer much improved communications, the Lord Mayor was against the idea for the usual reasons. In the end nothing happened because the City of London bribed Charles II with a loan of £100,000, which was a powerful argument, as the king was always short of money. In 1721 new proposals were put forward, including a Palladian bridge designed by Colen Campbell, but to no avail. Lobbying started again in 1736 and this time Nicholas Hawksmoor provided a

The modern Westminster Bridge, during its recent renovation.

design. There was still the usual opposition to a new bridge, but by now there was also more determination to make improvements to a London that was growing rapidly, in both size and importance, and in 1736 the Earl of Pembroke and his supporters were finally granted an Act to build one. Under the Act the watermen received £25,000 in compensation for loss of business and the Archbishop of Canterbury accepted £21,000. Under the terms of the Act, anyone found guilty of causing malicious damage to the new bridge would be treated as a felon and executed! During the construction, a number of watermen did cause damage to the bridge with their craft, either intentionally or accidentally, but malicious intent could not be proved and the sentence was never carried out.

Five locations were considered for the new bridge, including the site of the horse ferry itself, but the final choice was New Palace Yard, even though the purchase of land on both sides of the river at this point would be very expensive. The bridge was to be financed by a state lottery, and the novelist Henry Fielding dubbed it the 'Bridge of Fools', saying that its foundations were built on a gamble. In this he was to be proved right, as the first lottery failed to raise enough money and a further four unsuccessful lotteries were held. Finally, in 1741 the commissioners were forced to approach Parliament for a grant, and they were to request more money every year until the bridge was finished.

Various designs for a stone bridge had been submitted, but the commissioners favoured the cheaper option of a timber bridge. In 1738 a contract for building the stone piers only was given to the young Swiss engineer Charles Labelye, thus leaving open the option of whether the superstructure was to be of stone or wood. Instead

Valoué's horse-powered engine used to drive in the piles of the first Westminster Bridge.

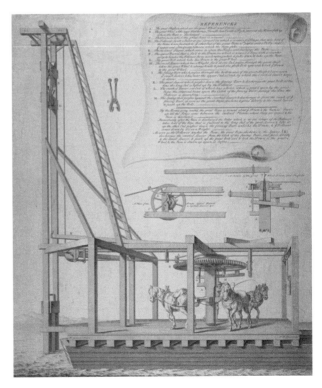

of using the traditional method of driving wooden piles into the riverbed, Labelye proposed using prefabricated boat-shaped caissons to support the piers. As we shall see, this was to cause a number of serious problems later on. The piles needed to protect the work were driven into the clay by a special machine invented by a Swiss watchmaker called James Valoué. Instead of using manpower, it used three horses, which walked round a windlass to lift a heavy weight, which was then released on to the pile. This saved an enormous amount of time, and by the end of October the caissons were in place and work could start on building the first two piers.

On 29 January 1739 the first stone was laid by the Earl of Pembroke and by 23 April the first pier was finished. That winter, with two piers completed, London suffered one of its most severe frosts and the Thames froze over for two months. A frost fair was set up on the ice, with printers' booths offering souvenirs and

The Thames during the Great Frost of 1739, a painting by Jan Griffier the Younger. The two piers of Westminster Bridge at the extreme right were a popular attraction and ladders allowed people to climb up onto them.

stalls selling food and drink. The two stone piers proved a particularly popular attraction, and ladders were set up against them for sightseers to climb up and enjoy the view. This can be clearly seen in a painting by Jan Griffier the Younger, now in the Guildhall Art Gallery.

During the delay the commissioners finally decided that the new bridge would be of stone, built to Labelye's design, which would be more expensive than a timber construction but would create a much finer adornment for London. There would be thirteen semicircular arches (though two extra arches were later added to the abutments), and the principal stone used would be from Portland and Purbeck. Work went well during the next few years. By the summer of 1742 the four central arches were complete and by spring 1744 all the piers and abutments were finished. In the autumn of 1746 the final stone was laid by the Earl of Pembroke, though the balustrade was not added until the following year.

In early 1747 the scientist William Watson spent a number of weeks using the bridge for one of his experiments to measure the speed of electricity. He stretched a wire from a Leyden jar across the bridge, with men at each end holding the wire and touching the water, so the current could travel across the bridge and back through the Thames.

Later that year disaster struck. There had been rumours of cracks in some of the arches as early as 1744, but during the summer of 1747 there were signs of movement in one of the piers. Labelye was not particularly concerned at first, but in September one of the stones fell into the Thames. Attempts were made to help the pier reach a firmer foundation by adding 700 tons of cannon balls, but it was soon clear that this was not working. It was then decided to strengthen the pier by adding piles around it and to reduce the weight on it with an ingenious structure of internal arches with hollow spaces underneath them. During 1749 the two arches were dismantled and the piles driven in, using Valoué's machine, the work being completed in December. In February 1750 there were two severe earth tremors in Westminster, but fortunately they caused no further damage to the bridge. By November the arches had finally been rebuilt and the bridge was officially opened on 18 November. Starting at midnight, the ceremony lasted two hours, with processions over the bridge and the singing of 'God save the King' over the central arch. For the rest of the day the bridge and river were full of activity, with curious sightseers keen to see the new wonder. The bridge became so crowded that, ironically, many were forced to hire a boat to get home.

After all his exertions, and with the bridge finally open, Labelye now planned to write a book about the building of the bridge, but he was never to get round to it. In 1752 he spent some time in the south of France for health reasons and lived the rest of his life in obscurity, dying in 1782.

The new bridge was not built in isolation but was part of a number of improvements in the Westminster area, as well as in the transport connections south of the river. The commissioners were granted powers to purchase all the property on the approaches to the bridge, and this allowed them to replace the narrow streets and squalid housing on the Westminster side with wide new streets, including Parliament Street, which was opened in 1756 and later extended to Charing Cross. The land on the Surrey side was mostly marshland and market gardens, and much of it belonged to the City and the Archbishop of Canterbury, who were able to negotiate a very good price for it. These purchases used up a large percentage of the funds available. The original estimate for a timber bridge had been £90,000, but the final cost of the stone bridge was around £390,000. As it was not a private

Westminster Bridge from the River, Looking South, British School, c. 1750. The image was probably inspired by a painting by Canaletto, though the anonymous British artist depicted the stone alcoves more accurately than the Italian master.

development, no tolls were ever charged, but the Government continued to pay for its maintenance and security.

Such was the popularity of the bridge that watchmen had to be employed, at first during the night, but later during the day as well, to stop people damaging the bridge or setting up stalls on it. The roadway needed regular repair and during the summer months it had to be watered to keep the dust down. The bridge was lit at night by thirty-two oil lamps, which were replaced in 1814 by gas lamps, and electric lighting was installed in 1898.

The finished bridge was considered to be a triumph and it attracted many artists to paint it, including Samuel Scott and William Marlow. But the most famous images of old Westminster Bridge were painted by Canaletto, who first arrived in London in 1746, probably attracted by the favourable early reports about the bridge. Because of the War of the Austrian Succession, English people were unable to travel in Europe, so the Venetian artist decided to come to the home of his greatest patrons, several of whom were among the bridge commissioners. Soon after his arrival he painted the first of many views of the new bridge, making the London river scene look very much like the Grand Canal in Venice. At this time the bridge was still incomplete, and Canaletto's bridge varies in several aspects from the finished structure. He included rather more stone alcoves than were erected, and placed statues of river gods over the central arch, an idea which had been considered but which was never carried out. These 'improvements' were repeated by the artist in later depictions of the bridge and were also copied by several other artists. He also painted a striking view of the City through one of the arches of the bridge, complete with its wooden centring, and a bucket hanging down from the parapet (see pages 10–11). In 1834, when the old Houses of Parliament were destroyed by fire, both Constable and Turner sketched the blaze, Constable from the bridge and Turner from a boat on the Thames. Turner produced two oil paintings of the subject, in which the old bridge features very prominently in the foreground.

Despite all the accolades, there were a few complaints, including the steepness of the bridge, which caused horses to slip as they crossed what was, essentially, a modern version of a medieval hump-backed bridge. The balustrades were also considered to be too high, so that one could get a good view only from the top of a carriage. Another problem reported in 1753 has a very modern ring to it. Apparently there was a 'great want of proper places to piss in at the four corners of the bridge. For the great numbers that piss there cause it to run down to the houses which make it very offensive'. To solve the problem, four stone basins were set up at each corner of the bridge. It seems that men urinating in public was not an unusual sight in eighteenth-century London, as can be seen in another of Canaletto's London pictures, *Old Horse Guards.*

One of the attractions of the new bridge was the echo under its arches, and it is claimed that people would float through the bridge playing the French horn to test it. Another curiosity was the fact that if you whispered into the wall of one of the alcoves on the bridge you could be heard clearly, through the traffic, from the alcove on the other side of the road. The alcoves had other uses, especially at night, and

Boswell used one in 1763 for one of his amorous encounters. As he said in his *Journal*, 'The whim of doing it there with the Thames rolling below us amused me much'.

While crossing the bridge in a carriage in 1802, Wordsworth was inspired by the view to write his famous sonnet *Upon Westminster Bridge*:

Earth has not anything to show more fair:
Dull would he be of soul who could pass by
A sight so touching in its majesty:
This City now doth like a garment wear

The beauty of the morning: silent, bare,
Ships, towers, domes, theatres, and temples lie
Open unto the fields, and to the sky,
All bright and glittering in the smokeless air.

Never did sun more beautifully steep
In his first splendour valley, rock, or hill;
Ne'er saw I, never felt, a calm so deep!

The river glideth at his own sweet will:
Dear God! The very houses seem asleep;
And all that mighty heart is lying still!

There is a plaque on the downstream side of the bridge commemorating the occasion of the poem's inspiration.

Despite all the euphoria over the new bridge, it was not long before problems became apparent. In 1759 two arches of London Bridge had been demolished to create a wider central arch, and this increased the flow of water, causing scouring that began to undermine the foundations of the piers of Westminster Bridge. When the old London Bridge was finally demolished in 1831 the problem grew worse. Reports were made by such eminent engineers as John Rennie, Thomas Telford and James Walker, all agreeing that the cause of the problem was Labelye's mistake in the way he laid the foundations. Various suggestions were made to solve the problem, including one from William Cubitt of paving the riverbed under the bridge to prevent further scouring. In 1843 James Walker attempted to strengthen the foundations of piers that were beginning to sink, as well as replacing some of the damaged stonework. To reduce the weight on the structure, the balustrades and alcoves were removed and replaced by a lower wall. But there were already calls to stop wasting money on repairs and to replace the bridge with a new one, one of the advocates being Charles Barry, the architect of the new Houses of Parliament going up alongside the bridge. In 1845 *Punch* said that 'Westminster-bridge is still very unwell. It looks really as if it were going to break up. Its celebrated echo, too, is very faint, and scarcely has sufficient strength left to answer when spoken to.'

In 1846 a Select Committee recommended that the bridge be replaced, but discussions continued for years about what type of bridge it should be and whether the new bridge should be on the same site or further downstream. In the meantime the bridge continued to be patched up, and it soon became a laughing stock, an editorial in *The Times* referring to it as 'a ruin one century old; too old to be safe, too young to be picturesque, and threatening any day to fall into the bed of the river'. There were also many complaints from those living and working in Lambeth, as the bridge was regularly closed to traffic while repairs were carried out, which forced them to take a detour to get to work, and it also affected trade in the shops of Westminster Bridge Road.

In April 1852 a parliamentary commission recommended that the old bridge be used as a temporary crossing while a new one was constructed as close as possible to it. The new bridge would be built with iron spans on stone piers and have no more than five arches, which would allow adequate headroom for vessels passing under it and still offer a reasonably easy incline for carriages going over it. An Act was passed in 1853, transferring the bridge to the Commissioners of Public Works, and allowing the new bridge to be built, with Thomas Page, the Commission's engineer, appointed to design it. This was Page's fourth bridge over the Thames, but it is the only one surviving, the others having been replaced. In 1854 the first pile was driven in, but the first contractors, Mare & Company, went out of business in September 1855 and work was suspended in March of the following year. Page agreed to take on the job of overseeing the project himself, and work restarted in 1857.

The bridge was built slightly upstream of the old bridge, not on the downstream side, as originally agreed. It is of seven iron spans, not the five originally specified, despite complaints from James Walker and others that this would not allow enough headway for river traffic; it seems that the needs of road traffic were already beginning to take precedence over those of the river traffic. At 85 feet wide, it is almost double the width of the old bridge. The arches are formed of iron ribs, mostly of cast iron, though, for greater strength, the flat crown of each arch is of wrought iron. The brick piers and abutments are faced in granite, and the abutments built using some of the Portland stone from the old bridge. Page made sure the foundations were robust by driving elm piles into the riverbed, and strengthening them with sheet iron and concrete. Charles Barry was taken on as architectural consultant, so that the new bridge would blend in with his new Houses of Parliament. Originally he had wanted the bridge to have Gothic pointed arches, but the final design was for much flatter, elliptical spans. The Gothic detailing on the cast-iron parapets and spandrels was made to Barry's designs and incorporates the coats of arms of England and Westminster.

There were many innovations in the way the bridge was built. Firstly, by using electric and gas lighting, they were able to work during all low tides, even during the night. Also, the job of fixing the bolts and placing the bags of concrete in the foundations was carried out by divers, while inspections were made from a diving bell. Most unusually, to save the expense of building a temporary bridge, the new bridge was constructed in two stages. The upstream side was built first, allowing the old bridge to be used by pedestrians and carriages during the construction. When that half was ready to be used, the old bridge was demolished and the downstream half completed. While awaiting the delayed arrival of some of the ironwork, four of the new piers were extended under the old arches, and this may well have helped the old bridge remain standing.

There were also delays in the creation of the approaches, but, eventually, in March 1860 the western half of the bridge opened to vehicles, while the old bridge continued to be used by pedestrians and those on horseback until the western part of it was demolished. There was a small ceremony in which Page and the Commissioner of Works walked over the bridge, followed by a crowd of boys. During the next twelve months the old bridge was removed and work on completing the new one moved ahead without delay. The official opening took place on Queen Victoria's birthday, 24 May 1862, at 3.45 a.m., the precise time of her birth. She had originally agreed to open the bridge in person but, as she was now in mourning for Prince Albert, who had died the previous year, she withdrew, and the event was low-key, with little ceremony. At 3.45 precisely a twenty-five-gun salute was fired in honour of the Queen's twenty-five years on the throne, and the barriers were opened for the public to cross.

As early as 1872 there were proposals to run horse-drawn trams over Westminster Bridge and along the new Embankment, though there was much opposition to the scheme, which was seen by some as being an underhand way of getting trams into the West End, whose richer inhabitants, who had their own carriages, considered the working-class trams to be a nuisance. Several attempts to get Parliamentary approval for the plan were made by the London Tramways Company and the London County Council, which took over responsibility for most of the tram network in 1899. Opposition also came from the City of Westminster and various omnibus companies, who were concerned about the competition, and there were also concerns about the tram service causing congestion on the bridge and its approaches. Approval was finally granted in 1906, allowing a circular route, which included Blackfriars Bridge, and was linked to the northern tram network via the Kingsway subway. The first part of the route, across Westminster Bridge and along the Embankment to a terminus on the north side of Blackfriars Bridge, opened in December 1906. The full service was delayed until September 1909, when the widened Blackfriars Bridge reopened.

Originally the bridge was painted bronze green, but during the Second World War it was repainted grey. In 1962, to celebrate its centenary, it was given a new coat of paint and in 1967 it was redecorated in green, gold, black and white. The predominant colour is green, which is the colour of the seating in the chamber of the House of Commons, which is located at this end of the Houses of Parliament.

Over the years a number of minor repairs have been carried out, but, despite the increase in traffic and especially the weight of modern vehicles, the bridge has survived with few problems. In 2003 Transport for London began a massive overhaul of the structure, including strengthening the piers to protect them from scour, and replacing the cast-iron fascias, which have received many knocks from river traffic. The latter work was carried out from floating cranes, and the bridge remained open during much of the work, which is due to be completed in 2009.

Westminster Bridge, because of its central location, has been the scene of many interesting events, some of national importance, others of a more ordinary, or

One of Westminster Bridge's ornate lamp standards, photographed before the recent renovations.

occasionally eccentric, nature. It was often used for the pageantry of royal weddings and coronations, when the bridge was specially decorated for the occasion, and in 1922 George V and Queen Mary crossed the bridge in an open carriage on their way to the opening of County Hall. It has also been a viewing point for significant events, such as the display of captured U-boats in 1918 and the sad procession of river boats up the Thames after the evacuation of Dunkirk in 1940. In August 1912 a seaplane piloted by Frank McClean caused quite a stir by flying under all the bridges from London to Waterloo before reaching Westminster Bridge. In 1953 sixty-one-year-old Major Draper, who had flown in both World Wars, ended up in court after an even more daring escapade. He flew a plane under fifteen of the eighteen bridges from Waterloo to Kew.

In 1893 it was feared that there had been an attempt to blow up the bridge when a 'bomb' was found on one of the pier buttresses, but it turned out to be an unexploded shell that its owner had tried to dispose of by dropping it into the Thames from the bridge. A rather more curious incident happened in 1899, when police found seventeen silver ingots and some silver cutlery on several of the pier abutments, so low down they could only be seen at low tide. The cutlery was found to be from a burglary, but the owners of the ingots were never found.

This curious little building by Westminster Pier was once used to measure the tides.

It has long been thought that the Romans crossed the Thames by a ford at Westminster, but there has never been any definite proof. In 1952 Lord Noel-Buxton decided to test the theory, and crowds lined the bridge to watch the attempt, but after walking halfway he was forced to swim the rest of the way. In 1967 another attempt was made by an accountant called Ian Spofforth, who was 7 feet 2 inches tall. He took an hour to walk across with the aid of a pole, and occasionally hanging on to a dinghy. Neither of them really proved anything, as the Thames at this point in Roman times was much wider and shallower than it is today.

Although security around Westminster, including the bridge, is now very strict, in previous decades the bridge was occasionally blocked by protesters trying to make a point by causing disruption. In 1980 a pacifist parked his car on the bridge and looked as if he was about to blow himself up, but it turned out to be a hoax. In 1990 a dozen gay campaigners padlocked themselves to a pink chain that was attached to both parapets of the bridge, and in 2004 banners were draped over the side of the bridge by campaigners for increased funding for research into myalgic encephalomyelitis (ME).

Today the bridge is usually thronged with visitors from all over the world, taking photographs of one another in front of Big Ben or views downriver of Hungerford Bridge and the London Eye. Few stop and

look at Thomas Thornycroft's dramatic bronze statue of Boudicca (or Boadicea) at the Westminster end of the bridge, erected there, somewhat controversially, in 1902. Boudicca was famous for leading a revolt against the Romans in AD 61, during which the city of *Londinium* was burnt to the ground. Below the statue, beside the pier, is a curious octagonal copper structure, which seems to serve no useful function. In fact, it once housed scientific instruments that were used to measure the tides.

At the Lambeth end of the bridge is the South Bank Lion, which has been here since 1966 but is much older. From 1837 it stood, painted bright red, on top of the Lion Brewery, which used to be where the Royal Festival Hall now stands. It was made of the artificial Coade stone, which is impervious to pollution, at Coade's Artificial Stone Manufactory, which was also based on the South Bank. During the Second World War the brewery was badly damaged and it was demolished to make way for the 1951 Festival of Britain. The lion was saved, however, on the instructions of George VI, and

Thornycroft's dramatic statue of Boadicea and her daughters at the north end of Westminster Bridge. The scythes on the chariot wheels are historically inaccurate.

99

The South Bank Lion, at the south end of Westminster Bridge, originally stood on top of the Lion Brewery, where the Royal Festival Hall now stands.

A drawing by Lawrence Wright of the Lion Brewery, made in 1949, shortly before the brewery demolished to make way for the Festival of Britain.

placed outside the entrance to Waterloo station. It was moved to its present location in 1966, when the station was redeveloped.

Because of its close proximity to the Houses of Parliament, Westminster Bridge has been much used as a film and television location. In a scene in the 1953 film *Genevieve* one of the cars in the London to Brighton veteran car run gets stuck in the tramlines, though, as the tramlines had already been removed, the scene was shot in Lewisham, with only background shots filmed on the bridge. (The run still takes place every November and the route still crosses the river at Westminster Bridge.) In the 1950 Boulting brothers' science-fiction film *Seven Days to Noon*, London is evacuated because of the threat of an atomic explosion, and they include a scene of an empty Westminster Bridge. A rather more dramatic use of the bridge occurred in Danny Boyle's 2002 thriller *28 Days Later*, in which the hero wakes up in St Thomas' Hospital to find that London has been decimated by a man-made virus, and he is seen walking around an empty city, including a deserted Westminster Bridge.

HUNGERFORD BRIDGE

THE present bridge is an oddly successful combination of an ugly nineteenth-century railway bridge with two modern hi-tech footbridges attached. Rather confusingly, the present structure is known by three different names. It is best known as the Hungerford Bridge, its original name, but it is also called the Charing Cross Railway Bridge after the railway station it serves. The new footways are officially known as the Golden Jubilee Bridges, though few people use the name.

The first bridge on the site was an elegant and popular suspension footbridge designed by Isambard Kingdom Brunel. It was built to serve the Hungerford Market on the north bank of the river, which had been built by Sir Edward Hungerford in 1682 on the site of the gardens of his family home, which had burned down in 1669. Selling fruit and vegetables, it was meant to compete with the more famous Covent Garden Market, but it was never a serious rival and nearly closed down in 1815. To give it a higher profile, Charles Fowler, architect of the central market building at Covent Garden, was commissioned to build a modern two-storey building, and in 1833 it opened with great celebrations, including a balloon ascent and a firework display.

The Hungerford Market Company later commissioned Brunel to build a bridge in the hope that it would attract new custom from south of the river. Brunel was still

Isambard Kingdom Brunel's elegant design for the Hungerford Suspension Bridge. Charles Fowler's classical market building can be clearly seen.

Isambard Kingdom Brunel (1806–59)

Isambard Kingdom Brunel is considered by many to be the greatest civil engineer of the nineteenth century. His father, Marc Isambard Brunel, was also an important engineer, but the son's career eclipsed that of his father. Born in Portsmouth, Isambard was educated in London and Hove, and then sent to France to study with a leading clockmaker, returning at the age of sixteen to finish his apprenticeship with his father. At this time his father was working on the construction of the first tunnel under the Thames, from Wapping to Rotherhithe, and Isambard became chief assistant engineer on the project. The tunnelling was highly dangerous and the Thames often broke through into the work, with much loss of life. Isambard was nearly killed during one such incident and took no further part in the project.

He spent part of his convalescence at Clifton in Bristol and became involved in the scheme to build a bridge across the Avon Gorge. At the second attempt his design was accepted, but he was never to see it built. Only the two towers had gone up before the money ran out, and no more work was carried out on it during his lifetime. It was built posthumously as his memorial and is probably his best-known work.

Through contacts made in Bristol, he carried out work in the city's docks, and this led to him being appointed engineer to the new Great Western Railway, which planned to build a line from London to Bristol. This was to be the greatest undertaking of his life, and for the next fifteen years he was the driving force of the operation, surveying the route, building viaducts and bridges as well as the Box Tunnel and Paddington station.

Brunel also designed three of the largest ships of his day. The *Great Western*, a wooden-hulled paddle steamer, was built to operate from Bristol to New York. When it proved a success, he built an even bigger vessel, the *Great Britain*, which was the first large iron ship – it was so large that they had to dismantle part of the lock for it to leave the dock. (After a long career, its rusty hull was returned to Bristol in 1970, where, after lengthy restoration, it is now a popular tourist attraction.) His largest ship, the *Great Eastern*, was built on the Isle of Dogs in London, where remnants of the slipway can still

Marochetti's statue of Isambard Kingdom Brunel stands in Temple Place, only a short distance from what is left of his bridge.

be seen. It was even more ambitious than the previous two, with two sets of engines, driving both paddles and screws. Its construction was fraught with difficulties, and two attempts had to be made to launch it into the Thames in 1858. It was never a commercial success but survived until 1888.

Somehow, with all these major schemes, he still found time for smaller ventures such as the elegant Hungerford Suspension Bridge in London. It is appropriate that, when it was demolished to make way for a railway bridge, the chains were used to complete his Clifton Suspension Bridge.

Brunel died at his home in London and was buried in the family vault in Kensal Green cemetery. The gravestone itself is surprisingly modest, but he is also commemorated by a statue on the Embankment, not far from the Hungerford Bridge. His youngest son, Henry Marc, was also an engineer and worked with Sir John Wolfe-Barry on Tower Bridge and the present Blackfriars Railway Bridge.

only twenty-nine, but he was already busy working on a number of major schemes, including the Clifton Suspension Bridge in Bristol, so he did not treat the bridge as being of any great importance. In 1835 he wrote in his diary: 'Suspension bridge across the Thames – I have condescended to be engineer of this, but I shan't give myself much trouble about it. If done it will add to my stock of irons.' Although it was to be a pedestrian rather than a vehicular bridge, and only 24 feet wide, it still offered a considerable challenge, as the Thames at this point was wider than the Avon Gorge, and Brunel's design included a number of innovations.

At 1,462 feet long, the bridge was one of the longest suspension bridges built at the time. It was of three spans, the central one of 676 feet, with two shore spans of 343 feet. To spread the load, Brunel built wide foundations to support the two massive brick and stone piers, out of which rose the Italianate towers. The suspension chains went through the top storey of the towers, running over saddles that rested on special rollers, lessening the effect of the horizontal pull on the towers' structure. There were two chains on each side, one above the other, and, to make the bridge as light as possible, he varied the thickness of the links.

Work started on building the bridge in 1841. The contractor was William Chadwick, who had worked with Brunel on his celebrated Maidenhead Railway Bridge, which had opened in 1839. The bridge opened with little ceremony on 1 May 1845, when, at 11.30 a.m., the directors and friends, along with about two hundred engineers and other important people, inspected the work. Prince Albert had had a private visit a few days earlier. At midday the general public were allowed on to the bridge and, according to *The Times*, over 35,000 people paid the halfpenny toll to cross it on the first day.

The bridge cost £102,000 to build but, although it proved to be a great success, Brunel was not paid for his work for at least a year. Ten thousand people paid the toll daily to cross the bridge, and these numbers grew with the opening of Waterloo station in 1848. The piers were also used as landing places for the steamboat companies, which offered popular trips on the Thames.

The 1840s marked the beginning of railway mania, so it is hardly surprising that as early as November 1845, only six months after the footbridge's successful opening, the London & Brighton Railway Company considered making an application to Parliament to build a railway over it to a new terminus on the north bank of the Thames. With the increase in traffic due to the opening of Waterloo station, the bridge's owners made attempts in 1857 to get permission from the Metropolitan Board of Works to allow vehicles to use it as well as pedestrians, but in the end it was the railways that got the upper hand. In 1859, the year Brunel died, an Act was passed allowing the Charing Cross Railway Company to build a railway line from London Bridge Station to a new terminus at Charing Cross, thus carrying its passengers right into the heart of the West End. (In 1861 they obtained the powers to build a similar bridge to a new terminus at Cannon Street, and this added greatly to the value of the Charing Cross scheme.) In 1860 the company purchased both bridge and market, the latter being the site for the new station. Although only a short extension, it was to prove very expensive to build because of the high cost of buying up the land along the route on which to build the viaducts. The governors of St Thomas' Hospital objected to losing a corner of their garden and forced the company to buy the whole site; they then moved the hospital to its present location opposite the Houses of Parliament.

The plans were generally met with approval as adding considerably to the convenience of travelling to and from London. As *The Times* said, 'To enter a station at Charing-cross and roll without interruption to Dover, seems almost too good to be true', adding that 'Frenchmen reaching London will find it pleasant to be set down so much nearer Leicester-square, and with less margin for the terrible extortion of our London cabmen'.

John (later Sir John) Hawkshaw, the South Eastern Railway's resident engineer, designed the new bridge, retaining Brunel's brick piers to save money, and adding four new cast-iron piers. Hawkshaw was also involved in the completion of Brunel's Clifton Suspension Bridge, and he arranged for the chains of Hungerford Bridge to be sold to the Clifton Suspension Bridge Company for use in the bridge over the Avon.

The bridge cost £180,000 to build and when it opened on 11th January 1864 it was much admired for its engineering. The new Charing Cross Railway Bridge made no pretence of being anything but a functional structure, with no claims to architectural excellence. It was a wrought-iron lattice-girder bridge of nine spans, each of the six river spans being of 154 feet. It was 1,360 feet long and 50 feet wide, and carried four lines of track. Two footways 7 feet wide were cantilevered on each side, and a toll was charged to pedestrians using them, though passengers using the steamboats did not pay. To allow access from the footbridge to the steamboat quays, staircases were cut into the piers, and the entrances can still be seen today. Tolls were charged on the footways until 1878, when the South Eastern Railway received £98,540 from the Metropolitan Board of Works to pay for their maintenance.

From 1860 trains crossed the Hungerford Bridge to and from Charing Cross Station. Attached to the bridge is a steamboat quay, with stairs cut into the bridge piers taking passengers up to the footbridge.

The bridge was declared free from toll, jointly with Waterloo Bridge, on 5 October in a low-key ceremony, when the key was handed over to a representative of the MBW and the turnstiles were removed.

By the time the bridge opened, the Victoria Embankment was being built as part of Bazalgette's great new sewage system, incorporating the Metropolitan District Railway as well as water and gas pipes. Hawkshaw had made allowances for the fact that the embankment would reach as far as Brunel's northern pier, especially as it was not possible to delay work on the bridge until the start of this major construction project. Today the pier stands hard against the footpath, evidence of the huge amount of land reclaimed for the Victoria Embankment. In 1882–8 the bridge was widened on the upstream side by Francis Brady, then the engineer for the South Eastern Railway. To do this, he widened Brunel's brick piers and added a further row of cast-iron piers, but the footway on that side was not replaced. In 1979 all the iron was replaced with steel in a major rebuilding scheme.

From the first, the bridge was considered to be an eyesore, even though Monet painted it many times and managed to make it look excitingly modern, albeit through a thick London fog. After the death of Edward VII in 1910, one of the many proposals for a suitable memorial to him was for a new road bridge at Charing Cross to replace the railway bridge, with Charing Cross station being resited on the south bank of the Thames. In 1916, and again in 1917, the railway company applied to Parliament for permission to strengthen the bridge to take the new, heavier trains, but the option was not taken up because of the introduction of electrification. This was a great relief for the many supporters of a new bridge, who included the architects Sir Aston Webb and Herbert Baker. However, the discussions and negotiations for the road bridge, which involved Parliament and the London County Council as well as a number of organisations, such as the Royal Institute of British Architects and the London Society, were to drag on for many years.

Many grand proposals were put forward, including one for a bridge that would double as a war memorial, with a 235-foot Tower of Victory on the site of Charing Cross station. There was even a design for a bridge with houses and shops down both sides, rather like old London Bridge, which would have been a useful source of revenue. Although many famous architects spoke out in favour of a new bridge, there were also those who defended the railway bridge, reminding people of the convenience of being able to arrive in the heart of London, rather than ending one's train journey at Waterloo and having to makes one's own way across the river. In 1924 George Bernard Shaw entered the fray with a letter to *The Times*. Of the railway bridge he admitted that 'its appearance has never cost me a tear or a sleepless night', yet pointed out, with his usual dry humour, that 'the necessity for another first-rate bridge at Charing Cross is so obvious that anyone who does not see it must be dismissed as in a condition of hypnotic obsession with the existing Hungerford footbridge and its attached railway'.

By the time the Royal Commission on Cross-River Traffic in London considered the problem in 1926, as part of a much wider look at London's bridges, the future of an ailing Waterloo Bridge had been added to the equation. If a road bridge were to be built at Charing Cross, this would take pressure off Rennie's Waterloo Bridge and allow it to be repaired. Various options were considered, and the Commission's report recommended that a steel double-decker road and rail bridge be built to replace the Hungerford Bridge This would mean moving Charing Cross station to a site slightly to the east but also allow Waterloo Bridge to be widened, rather than demolished.

The Government asked for the proposal to be looked at by a committee of engineers, who rejected it and offered a cheaper alternative plan, recommending Charing Cross station be moved to the south bank of the Thames, a suggestion first put forward nearly twenty years earlier. During the next few years the Government held negotiations with the London County Council and the railway company, and a number of new schemes, or modifications of old ones, were put forward, all of which were the subject of heated debate among professional bodies such as the Royal Academy, the Royal Institute of British Architects and the Town Planning Institute. The government claimed that the scheme was of national importance, and that the work would create new jobs at a time of high unemployment, but the main problems related to the siting of the approaches and the new station, as well as the potential traffic problems. In 1930 the LCC presented a Bill to Parliament, which received a second reading, but at the committee stage the LCC's plan was rejected, though the committee still believed the construction of the bridge to be an important improvement.

The LCC revised the scheme again and were planning to promote a new Bill in Parliament, but the Transport Minister, Herbert Morrison, announced that the Government was unable to provide money from the Road Fund to cover the promised 75 per cent of the cost of building the new bridge and restoring Waterloo Bridge. The grandiose Charing Cross Bridge scheme was finally dead and, although several attempts were made to resurrect the scheme in the next few years, even after the Second World War, it was never to be. Despite so much agreement on the nature of the problem, the many interested parties were finally unable to find a solution. The fate of Waterloo Bridge was also sealed by the decision, but that is another story, told in the next chapter.

Not even the Luftwaffe could destroy the Hungerford Bridge. During an air raid in 1941 Charing Cross station was hit, and a parachute mine landed on the bridge but failed to explode. During a complicated and dangerous six-hour operation, Lieutenant Gidden managed to defuse the bomb and was later awarded the George Cross for his bravery. In June 1944 a V1 flying bomb hit the bridge, knocking out two lines, but it was back in operation by the following day.

For visitors to the 1951 Festival of Britain on the South Bank, a Bailey bridge was erected on the upstream side of the railway bridge by the Royal Engineers, but it was dismantled afterwards. For Queen Elizabeth II's coronation in 1953 the full length of the bridge was decorated with a painting of an old train with a lion as engine-driver. For many years the narrow and gloomy footbridge on the downstream side of the bridge was the only way visitors could get across the river to the new attractions on the South Bank, and it was always an unpleasant experience, with the screeching trains only feet away from you. But that was about to change.

In 1996 a competition was held for new footbridges to be added to each side of the bridge. The competition was won by Lifschutz Davidson and the engineers WSP, and work began in 2000. The new construction was a very complex operation, made more complicated by the fact that the Northern and Bakerloo Underground lines ran under the Thames at this point, and there was also a fear that there may have been unexploded Second World War bombs on the riverbed, which meant some of the foundations had to be dug by hand. This problem led to the designs being modified and added hugely to the cost of the project, which was fortunately bailed out by London's new Mayor, Ken Livingstone, who was able to provide the extra £16.7 million required.

The three 225-ton concrete beams that support the footbridges were towed upriver by barges, an impressive sight attracting many spectators, and were dropped into place using cranes and divers. The walkways themselves are 984-foot concrete decks, attached by steel cables to a forest of leaning suspension masts. The upstream bridge was completed and opened in May 2002. Then the old downstream footbridge was removed and that side built, the work being finished by September. The bridges were officially opened in July 2003 by Princess Alexandra and were named the Golden Jubilee Bridges to commemorate the Queen's fifty years on the throne.

The total cost of construction was £40 million, but the result is a complete triumph. London has gained two attractive pedestrian river crossings offering wonderful views in both directions, and the large numbers using them indicate that

Hungerford Bridge in the twenty-first century, with the pair of Golden Jubilee Bridges attached to it.

people feel they are great places to be. They are popular with Londoners and visitors alike, offering good links from the West End to the regenerated South Bank, and they look particularly striking at night, when they are illuminated. They also have the benefit of drawing one's attention away from the ugly old railway bridge, though you can now appreciate Brunel's restored piers at close quarters. There are lifts at both ends of the bridges, so they are fully accessible for those with mobility difficulties. The only inconvenience is that it is not possible to cross from one side to the other except at the two ends. There were plans to open up a passageway through the Surrey pier, but this was not carried out and it is unlikely now that it ever will be.

On the south side of the bridge is the Royal Festival Hall, a concert hall that is all that remains of the Festival of Britain. It is now the heart of the South Bank Centre, which includes the Hayward Gallery, the Queen Elizabeth Hall and the Purcell Room. After a £90 million renovation, the Royal Festival Hall reopened in the summer of 2007, with improved acoustics and better facilities. There are lots of shops, cafes and restaurants in and around the complex, making it a lively place to visit. On the north bank is the 'new' Charing Cross station. In the late 1980s it was redeveloped, with the dramatic office block, Embankment Place, designed by Terry Farrell, being built over the platforms.

The wide decks of the Golden Jubilee Bridges are popular with Londoners and visitors, offering fine views up and down the river.

WATERLOO BRIDGE

BUILT on a wide bend in the river, Waterloo Bridge is the longest bridge in London. It also has some of the finest views in London, with splendid vistas in each direction, upstream towards the Gothic towers of the Houses of Parliament and downstream to the baroque dome of St Paul's Cathedral surrounded by the many skyscrapers of the modern City.

The first bridge was built by the Strand Bridge Company, which was formed in 1809 to build a new crossing from a site just west of Somerset House to the Lambeth shore. An Act of Parliament allowed them to raise £500,000 in shares and to borrow £300,000 more, a huge amount of money to invest in such a project. The decision to build a level bridge rather than the traditional humped variety meant that they had to build long approach roads on both sides of the river, which added greatly to the costs. The company commissioned a design from George Dodd, a young but able engineer, and for many years it was thought that his design was the one that was built. It would seem, however, that the commissioners had doubts about the design and asked the more experienced John Rennie to take a look at it, and he was then asked to put forward a design of his own. Rennie offered two designs, one of seven spans and another of nine, and the directors accepted the cheaper second option. The design is very similar to that of a much shorter bridge Rennie had built in 1803 at Kelso in

The Opening of Waterloo Bridge, Whitehall Stairs *by John Constable. In the foreground, the Prince Regent boards the royal barge at Whitehall to be taken to the bridge for the ceremony.*

Scotland, and which still spans the Tweed today. Dodd was kept on and worked on the bridge as Rennie's assistant. The work was carried out by the contractors Jolliffe & Banks, who had already worked with Rennie on other projects and were later to work with him on Southwark Bridge and London Bridge.

The first pile was driven in on 1 March 1811 and the foundation stone was laid on 11 October by the company's chairman, Henry Swann MP. Work on the bridge went well, but the acquisition of land to build the approaches proved costly and time-consuming. The bridge had nine elliptical spans of 120 feet and it was 42 feet wide, with a footpath 7 feet wide on each side. The whole bridge was faced with Cornish granite and the balustrades were of granite from Aberdeen. On each pier was a pair of Doric columns, and above them was an alcove that offered refuge to pedestrians. The four tollhouses were also in Doric style, and they housed a novelty, turnstiles, which allowed the tollkeepers to control the passage of pedestrians, while at the same time recording the number of people passing through.

In 1816 the company asked Parliament for permission to rename the bridge in honour of Wellington's victory against Napoleon at Waterloo in 1815. The bridge was opened by the Prince Regent in a magnificent ceremony on 18 June 1817, the second anniversary of the battle. The riverbanks were lined with vast crowds, the river was full of ceremonial barges and there were flags everywhere. The Prince left Whitehall in a state barge, followed by the Lord Mayor's barge and various others. To the sound of gun salutes, the barge went through the central arch of the bridge and moored at the Surrey end of it. Accompanied by the Duke of York and the Duke of Wellington, the Prince then processed across the bridge, which was lined with Waterloo veterans, before returning to Whitehall by barge. After the opening, the Prince Regent offered a knighthood to Rennie, which he turned down.

The artist John Constable was probably present at the opening of the bridge and made a number of sketches at the time. He planned to show a large painting of the opening at the Royal Academy in 1820, but he put it to one side and did not return to the subject for several years. He started a new version in 1829 and the finished picture was exhibited at the Royal Academy in 1832, to mixed reviews. This striking and, for Constable, unusual urban landscape is now in Tate Britain, and there are several other versions, one of which can be seen at Anglesey Abbey in Cambridgeshire.

The bridge was greatly admired, and Canova, the great Italian sculptor, who was on a visit to England, called it 'the noblest bridge in the world, worth a visit from the remotest corner of the earth'. M Dupin, a Frenchman, called it a 'colossal monument worthy of Sesostris and the Caesars'. Despite all the plaudits, however, it was not a commercial success, and the shareholders were never to make a profit. Part of the problem was that it was a toll bridge, and people preferred to go the long way round, using the free bridges at Blackfriars and Westminster. The other reason was that the bridge did not really lead anywhere very important, as the Lambeth side was still mostly undeveloped. The finances improved with the coming of the railways and the opening of Waterloo station in 1848, as the bridge was the quickest route to the station, and extra tollkeepers had to be employed. However, toll revenue fell again when penny omnibus services began to operate from the station to the Strand in the 1860s, using the bridges at Blackfriars or Westminster.

This engraving of Waterloo Bridge was made by J. Greig for Walks Through London, *published in 1817, the year the bridge was opened.*

A bizarre and very public death occurred on the bridge in 1841. Samuel Scott, a twenty-seven-year-old entertainer and athlete known as the 'American Diver', announced that he would be diving from Waterloo Bridge on 11 January. Famed for extraordinary diving feats in his homeland, he had already performed at Rotherhithe, so large crowds lined the bridge and the riverbanks to await his arrival. Dressed only in a shirt and trousers, he climbed on to the scaffolding and began his performance by putting his feet in a noose and hanging upside down. He then put his neck in the noose and said he would 'dance upon air before I dive', a feat he had performed many times before. After he had been hanging for several minutes people realised something was wrong and he was cut down and taken to Charing Cross Hospital, where, despite attempts to revive him, he died.

In 1857 someone used the bridge under cover of darkness to dispose of a murder victim by lowering a carpet bag full of body parts by rope into the Thames. Owing to a misjudgement, the bag ended up on one of the piers and was discovered by a pair of young watermen early the next day; thinking they had found treasure, they had an unpleasant shock when they opened it. The murderer was never found.

From as early as the 1850s there were calls for the bridge to be made toll-free, and plans were put forward in 1864, but it was not until the 1870s that the matter was seriously considered as part of a move by the Metropolitan Board of Works to free all London's bridges from toll. Waterloo Bridge was freed by the MBW in a brief ceremony at midday on 5 October 1878, and many people queued to be among the first to cross it. The footbridges on Cannon Street and Charing Cross railway bridges were freed on the same day. The Waterloo Bridge Company had claimed £750,000 in compensation, but was forced to accept £475,000. In the following seven months it was estimated that the traffic over the bridge nearly doubled.

The Freeing of Waterloo Bridge. The tolls on London's bridges were very unpopular, so vast crowds turned up to see them freed from toll and to be the first to cross them.

In 1878 electric street lighting was tested on Victoria Embankment, and in the following year the experiment was extended to Waterloo Bridge, where ten lights were installed, the power being supplied by a French company, the Société Générale d'Electricité. These were among the first London thoroughfares to be lit by electricity, and the experiment was considered to be a success, though the system used proved to be rather expensive, and the scheme was abandoned. Electric lighting was permanently installed on the bridge in 1897, but the replacement of the original lamp standards, said to have been made from captured French cannon, caused an outcry in some quarters.

An engineer's report to the MBW in 1880 noted that the foundations of the bridge needed to be deepened to make it more secure. Ironically, it was Rennie's new London Bridge, which had opened in 1831, which caused the problem, allowing the river to flow faster, with the increased scouring exposing the foundations. Between 1882 and 1884 £62,000 was spent in putting a wall of steel piles round each pier and filling in the space with concrete.

Trams had been operating in London since the 1870s, but only in the outer areas. Not until 1908 were the networks north and south of the river able to link up, with the building of the Kingsway subway extension, which tunnelled under Aldwych and the Strand, passed through the brick arches underneath Rennie's approach road to Waterloo Bridge, and emerged from a tunnel on to the Embankment. From here the trams travelled along the Embankment, crossing the Thames by Blackfriars and Westminster Bridges. At first the subway could take only single-decker trams, but in 1930 the tunnel was rebuilt to take double-deckers.

When one considers all the plaudits heaped on the bridge, in praise of its classical looks, it seems odd that so few artists of note chose to depict it during its heyday. Constable, as we have seen, celebrated its opening, and in 1896 Whistler produced a number of fine lithographs of it from his room at the Savoy Hotel. Between 1899 and 1901, Monet made three visits to London, also staying at the Savoy. Monet was particularly attracted to London because of its fog and one of the aims of his visits was to 'paint some effects of fog on the Thames'. From his window he painted about forty pictures of Waterloo Bridge, at different times of day and in different lights. He also portrayed the heavy industry on the south bank of the river, whose smoking chimneys contributed to the 'smog' he so enjoyed painting.

In December 1923 one of the piers near the centre of the bridge showed signs of subsidence, which was serious enough for the London County Council to consider rebuilding it, and so began a ten-year battle between those who wished to save the bridge and those intent on replacing it. Proposals to widen the bridge, because of the growth in traffic, prompted the first of many letters to *The Times* from well-known architects, artists and writers, complaining that it would cause 'lasting disfigurement' to the bridge. There were also complaints from the Port of London Authority, which pointed out that, as the bridge was on a bend, it was already difficult to navigate the narrow arches, and that widening the bridge would make it more dangerous for river traffic. George Bernard Shaw, however, claimed that 'The wave of enthusiasm for the inviolable beauty of Waterloo Bridge has not carried me away. The bridge is not only too narrow for the traffic … but for its length and dignity. It will be enormously improved aesthetically by being widened.'

In April 1924 the LCC took the decision to rebuild and widen the bridge, and plans were made to erect a temporary bridge alongside it. They hoped to keep the bridge open until this was installed, but in May further subsidence forced the LCC to close the bridge to carry out emergency repairs. This involved taking up part of

One of Monet's many paintings of Waterloo Bridge, depicting its many moods at different times of day. This one, painted in 1900, is called Waterloo Bridge, Cloudy Day. *The south side of the river was still very industrial.*

the roadway to reduce the load on the sinking pier, and building supports for the arches on either side of it. On 30 June the bridge was reopened for pedestrians only. On 14 July the bridge was reopened to vehicular traffic, including buses, but with a weight limit of 10 tons, and a speed limit of 3 mph over the site of the subsidence, where the roadway had been replaced with a timber surface. A temporary bridge was now begun on the downstream side of the ailing bridge, and as close as possible to it, so as to make use of the approach roads. To make it easier for river traffic to pass through, the central span of the temporary bridge was the width of two of the bridge spans. The steel spans were built on the old bridge and lowered into place by crane at night. During May and June 1925 the old bridge was closed to vehicles to allow the 500-ton central span to be constructed on it and lifted into position. In August the public witnessed a curious spectacle as thirty buses, each one filled with 6 tons of sandbags to represent a full load of passengers, were used to test the temporary bridge prior to its opening. When it opened on 12 August it carried all the southbound traffic, with all northbound vehicles using the old bridge.

In February 1925 the LCC recommended the construction of a completely new bridge, with no more than five spans, and wide enough for six lanes of traffic. This decision caused a huge outcry from the usual quarters and yet more letters to *The Times.* One letter of protest came, somewhat ironically, as we shall see, from the architect, Giles Gilbert Scott, who said that 'The proposed destruction of Waterloo Bridge fills one with dismay and calls for the strongest possible protest'. Such criticism clearly had its effect, at least in the short term, as the LCC now commissioned a report from the architect Sir Edwin Lutyens about the artistic effect of widening the existing bridge to take four lanes of traffic. He looked at a number of options but was unable to come up with any design that did not seriously damage the appearance of the bridge. The Council also looked again at the possibility of underpinning the old bridge, but they decided against it, and in early 1926 announced a competition for the design of a new bridge. By now another two piers were showing signs of settlement.

Throughout all these disputes and arguments there were many earnest letters on the subject to *The Times* from architects and engineers, but there were also some lighter moments. One letter tells the story of a friend saying to an engineer 'How sad it is to see one of Wren's masterpieces being ruthlessly torn down', to which the engineer replies, unwilling to expose his friend's ignorance: 'Yes, but we engineers, in our affectionate way, call him Rennie.' George Bernard Shaw again played devil's advocate in a letter to *The Times* of 3 May 1928. He described Waterloo Bridge as 'a causeway with holes in it, blocking the view of the river hopelessly… For 30 years I have lived with Waterloo Bridge under my study windows; and my hatred of its incurable ugliness and fundamental wrongness increased during all that time… All that is needed for Waterloo Bridge is a sufficiency of dynamite, followed by a law making it a capital offence to make perforated causeways across the Thames.' Rennie must have been turning in his grave.

The survival of Rennie's bridge ultimately depended on the result of the ongoing 'Battle of the Bridges' about the provision of new bridges over the Thames to cope with the increase in London's traffic. The key to the problem lay in the plans for a road bridge to replace the Charing Cross Railway Bridge, which would take pressure off Waterloo Bridge. In 1926 the Government set up a Royal Commission on Cross-River Traffic to look at all the issues, and the LCC put off their rebuilding plans until it reported its findings. Its recommendation was for a new road bridge at Charing Cross, and for Waterloo Bridge to be retained, with its foundations strengthened by underpinning and its roadway widened. The problem for the LCC was that, while the Government had offered to provide 75 per cent of the cost of rebuilding Waterloo Bridge, there was no such financial commitment for the new Charing Cross Bridge. In 1929 a government grant for the Charing Cross Bridge was offered, but this was withdrawn in 1931, and the LCC voted again to demolish the old Waterloo Bridge and replace it with a new one, choosing Sir Giles Gilbert Scott, who had earlier defended Rennie's bridge, to design it.

But even this was still not the end of the matter. The LCC had to get Parliament's approval and the provision of a grant from the Road Fund, but this was not forthcoming. When the Government offered to provide 60 per cent of the cost of reconditioning the old bridge, the LCC reluctantly agreed, and during 1933 tenders were invited for the work to be carried out. A few months later, with Herbert Morrison the newly elected Leader, the Council decided that the debate had been going on long enough and decisive action was required. Morrison had been pushing for a new bridge since 1924, saying that what London needed was a bridge, not a monument, and he was now determined to get his way. The bridge had been a political football for too long and so, when Parliament again refused to support the Council's plans financially, it decided to go it alone, with the cost, about £1,295,000, coming from the rates.

On 20 June 1934, more than ten years after the controversy began, the bridge's demolition began with a brief ceremony, in which Herbert Morrison helped to remove the first stone from the old bridge. Two days later, the bridge was closed to all traffic, and demolition of the balustrades began. The demolition was a complicated procedure, especially of the arches, and the job took three years to complete.

Public affection for the old bridge was enormous, and parts of the structure were offered for sale. The 1,300 granite balusters were sold off at £1 each; one of them is known to have been re-used as a sundial in a garden in Dorking. A short section of the balustrade was given to the London Museum (now the Museum of London). Parts of the bridge found their way to different parts of the Commonwealth, including lamp standards to Rhodesia, four stones to Australia to be used in a new bridge, and a 2½-ton block of granite to New Zealand, where it was incorporated into the new Parliament building in Wellington. 10 tons of the granite were taken to Australia as ballast and were used in a town hall built in the 1960s. The LCC even used some of the granite in an extension to County Hall.

The elm piles, well seasoned from spending over a hundred years in the Thames mud, were particularly popular. A coach of the 'Coronation Scot', a new express train, was panelled with it, and it was also used to furnish the captain's room of the ocean-going liner *Queen Elizabeth*. Rooms in Toynbee Hall and the new *Times* building were panelled with it, and the bookshelves in the library of Anglesey Abbey in Cambridgeshire were made from it, which is particularly apt, as a version of

A postcard of Waterloo Bridge from the 1930s, showing the temporary iron bridge alongside while the bridge's future was decicded.

Constable's *The Opening of Waterloo Bridge* now hangs there. Smaller souvenirs were also available, including cigarette boxes from Fortnum & Mason and a tea table from a shop in Wigmore Street, whose sales pitch included the line: 'Its pleasing colour is due to its 60 years' [sic] immersion in Thames mud.'

In 1936, by which time most of the bridge had been demolished, it was suggested that part of the bridge should be used as a memorial to Rennie in his native Scotland. The remaining stone was not suitable, but a member of the public, who had bought two balusters, donated one of them for the monument, which now stands on a site overlooking Phantassie Farm in East Linton, where he was born. The memorial takes the form of a seat made from local stone, inlaid with a bronze medallion of the engineer. In the centre is the baluster, with a sundial on top. Two of the bridge's lamp standards were given to Kelso in the Scottish Borders and still stand at one end of the bridge Rennie built there in 1803.

While the bridge was being demolished, the Council continued to press the Government for a contribution towards the new bridge, and in late 1937 it finally relented, offering to provide 60 per cent of the cost from the Road Fund. Meanwhile the design of the bridge was being fine-tuned, and a number of changes were made to Scott's original ideas. It was to be 80 feet wide, nearly twice as wide as Rennie's bridge, so it could take six lanes of traffic. It would have five arches of 238 feet each, almost twice the size of Rennie's, with the first one on the north bank spanning the Embankment. It would be made of reinforced concrete, with the piers faced with granite and the superstructure with Portland stone, to blend in with neighbouring buildings such as Somerset House.

Work started in early 1938, and it was estimated that the bridge would be finished some time in 1940. On 4 May 1939 a new foundation stone, cut from the old one, was laid without ceremony in the north abutment. With the outbreak of war, work on the bridge was much delayed, because of a shortage of materials and manpower. As so many men were away fighting the war, many of the workers were women, and for this reason the bridge earned the nickname of the 'Ladies' Bridge'. During the war the bridge was hit about twenty times by enemy bombs, which caused further delays. The bridge was partially opened to traffic on 11 August 1942, with one lane only in each direction. Pedestrians had to continue using the temporary bridge until December. The bridge opened fully on 21 November 1944 and was officially declared open by Herbert Morrison in a low-key ceremony on 10 December 1945.

In order to deal with the expected increase in traffic, it had been planned to build a large roundabout at the junction with the Strand, and the Lyceum Theatre was bought up by the LCC. It was forced to close in 1939 so it could be demolished, but the scheme was dropped and the theatre was able to reopen in 1940. Another project that never reached fruition was for the installation of sculptures at the four corners of the bridge, and plinths were provided for them. Charles Wheeler was asked to make sculptures of the Four Winds, but the offer was later withdrawn. In 1947 the Council held a competition, and Barbara Hepworth, Frank Dobson and Eric Kennington submitted designs. None of them was considered suitable, so Waterloo Bridge still has its four 'empty plinths' above the staircases at each end. (For a few months in 2007 the bridge did host a pair of statues in the form of Antony Gormley's bronze casts of his naked body, installed there during an exhibition of his work at the Hayward Gallery.)

By the early 1950s trams were being phased out, and the Kingsway subway became obsolete after the last tram passed through it in 1952. It was later converted into an underpass by extending it on to Waterloo Bridge to allow northbound traffic to avoid the busy Strand intersection, opening in 1964. The exit from the tunnel where the trams emerged on to the Embankment has now been converted into a bar and restaurant.

After the Second World War it was decided to hold an event that, it was hoped, would revive the nation's spirits. The site chosen was the area between Waterloo and Hungerford Bridges on the south bank of the Thames, which had once been industrial but was now largely derelict. The Festival of Britain was held there in 1951, with its focus being the Royal Festival Hall. The hall remained as a permanent feature and was the catalyst for the development of the area into what is now known as the

The present Waterloo Bridge, with Somerset House in the background.

South Bank. In 1957 the National Film Theatre (now renamed BFI Southbank) opened underneath the southern end of Waterloo Bridge, and the Queen Elizabeth Hall, Purcell Room and Hayward Gallery were added in the 1960s. To the east of the bridge is the Royal National Theatre, which opened in 1976. The space under the southern arch of the bridge is now occupied by a second-hand book market, which is yet another attraction in what is becoming a very lively part of London.

In September 1978 an extraordinary event that could have come straight out of a James Bond novel took place on the bridge. Georgi Markov, a Bulgarian exile working for the BBC Overseas Service, was waiting at a bus stop at the south end of the bridge when a passing stranger stabbed him in the thigh with an umbrella, got into a taxi and sped off. That night Markov had a high fever and was taken to hospital, and four days later he was dead. Before he died, he mentioned the incident to his wife, and later investigation discovered a tiny metal ball, no bigger than a pinhead, in his thigh. There were two holes in it, which had been filled with the deadly poison ricin. Markov was a journalist who had been openly critical of the Bulgarian regime, and he had been warned to stop broadcasting or he would be poisoned, but the method used to silence him was highly unusual. For years the Bulgarian authorities denied any involvement, but it is now accepted that the attack was carried out by a Bulgarian secret agent, Francesco Giullino, using a KGB-created weapon.

Many of London's bridges have featured in films, but Waterloo is the only bridge to have given its name to a film. Based on Robert Sherwood's sentimental play of the same name, the first *Waterloo Bridge*, directed by James Whale, was filmed entirely in Hollywood and opened in 1931. A second version, starring Vivien Leigh and Robert Taylor, was filmed in London in 1940, and claims have been made that some of it was actually filmed on the bridge, but this is unlikely, as it was still under construction. The story tells of a young ballet dancer, Myra, who meets a young army officer called Roy on the bridge during the First World War. They fall in love and decide to marry, but he is sent to the front and is later reported killed in action. She loses her job and works as a prostitute, only to meet Roy when he returns at the end of the war. They arrange to marry, but Myra feels so ashamed about her recent past that she returns to Waterloo Bridge, where she commits suicide by jumping under an army truck.

When the new bridge was being built, two of the columns and a piece of the balustrade from Rennie's bridge were incorporated into the south abutment of the new bridge, but these disappeared when the South Bank was redeveloped. However, part of the old bridge can still be seen, though it is easily overlooked. Under the northern arch, on the river side of the Embankment, is a platform that was built on top of one of the original piers, and the bases of the Doric columns can be seen on both sides. Standing on the Platform gives one a very good idea of just how narrow the old bridge was compared to the new one.

WATERLOO SUICIDES

For centuries people have been committing or attempting to commit suicide from London's bridges. The tide is so fast-flowing that few people jumping or even falling into the Thames have survived. Bridges were also a refuge for the extreme poor, as many of the homeless and destitute would spend the night huddled under the arches of bridges, as is shown in an engraving by Gustave Doré. During the nineteenth century, and particularly after 1840, *The Times* was full of reports of inquests or court cases relating to suicide attempts, as it was legally a crime and was often referred to as 'self-murder'. Some of the stories are heart-rending, often about women whose husbands had died, leaving them destitute, women who had arrived in London looking for work and been seduced and abandoned, or men whose businesses had failed. Even sadder are those stories of women so desperate that they throw their children into the river before jumping in themselves. Although the courts sometimes treated attempted suicides with kindness and understanding, their fate was often the workhouse or a further, usually successful, attempt at suicide.

Blackfriars and Westminster Bridges, being free, were much frequented by suicides, but Waterloo Bridge had the unenviable reputation of being the most popular one of all. In the 1840s about 15 per cent of London's suicides were from Waterloo Bridge, probably because, as a toll bridge, it was less busy than the others, and they were less likely to be disturbed. Ironically, a director of the bridge company was later to say that 'the tolls surely saved many a penniless wretch from flinging himself into the dark, cold waters'. In 1873 the Royal Humane Society set up a twenty-four-hour 'receiving house' by the northern end of the bridge, manned by a doctor who would attempt to revive any victims brought to him, and in 1875 alone twenty-one people were saved by this method.

The Waterloo Bridge suicides inspired a number of artists, novelists and playwrights, who portrayed fallen women being redeemed through the act of drowning. Such paintings and plays may well have played a part in shaping the bridge's undeserved reputation as far more suicides took place in the Serpentine than from Waterloo Bridge. Thomas Hood's 1844 poem *The Bridge of Sighs*, though based on the real story of Mary Furley, who tried to commit suicide in the Regent's Canal, moves the scene to Waterloo Bridge, depicting her as a seduced and abandoned woman:

Gustave Doré's engraving Under the Arches *shows London's desperate poor sheltering under a bridge, probably London Bridge.*

George Frederic Watts'
powerful painting, Found
Drowned, *shows a young*
suicide victim under the
arch of Waterloo Bridge. It
may have been inspired by
Thomas Hood's poem,
The Bridge of Sighs.

One more unfortunate,
Weary of breath,
Rashly importunate,
Gone to her death!

So popular was the poem that, when Hood died, a bas-relief based on it decorated his memorial in Kensal Green Cemetery, though this has since been stolen. During the following decades other writers would also refer to the bridge as the 'Bridge of Sighs'.

Many artists were inspired by Hood's poem, including G. F. Watts, who, in *Found Drowned*, shows a suicide victim, a beautiful young woman, lying peacefully under an arch of the bridge by moonlight, her body arranged in the form of a cross. A victim of drowning would in reality have looked soiled and bloated, but the beauty of the woman emphasised the symbolism of redemption. In 1848 George Cruikshank produced a series of etchings called *The Drunkard's Children*. The story tells of the effects of drinking gin, and in particular of the fate of a drunkard's son who is convicted of a robbery, and the despair of his sister, who, in the final and most striking image, jumps to her death from Waterloo Bridge. In 1858 a selection of Hood's poems was published, with etchings by prominent artists; to accompany *The Bridge of Sighs*, John Everett Millais produced a sombre nocturnal image of a young woman standing in front of the bridge, holding a child in a heavy cloak.

The subject was also a popular one in the theatre. W. T. Moncrieff's *The Scamps of London* from 1843 and Charles Selby's *London by Night*, first performed in 1844, both had an actress drowning after a leap from the bridge, and both plays were so popular they were revived on and off for forty years. At the first performance of Edward Stirling's *The Bohemians* in 1843, which included another suicide, the principal actress missed the mattress in her plunge from the bridge and was seriously injured.

BLACKFRIARS BRIDGE

IN the 1750s the City of London decided to build a grand new entrance to the City in the form of a bridge at Blackfriars. In 1759 it held a competition for a design for the new bridge, which attracted sixty-nine entries, including plans from John Smeaton, George Dance the elder, Sir William Chambers and John Gwynn, all seasoned engineers and architects. At first Gwynn's design was favoured, but in the end it was the innovative plans by Robert Mylne, an unknown architect aged twenty-six, which were chosen. Mylne was a confident and ambitious young Scotsman, who had been born into a family of masons and architects. He had just returned from four years in Rome, where he had won first prize for architecture at the prestigious Academy of St Luke. When he heard about the competition for the new bridge, he could not resist the challenge, despite his lack of experience in the face of competition from so many renowned and experienced masters.

His design made the shortlist of fourteen, and there followed a heated debate about his choice of elliptical arches instead of the traditional semicircular ones, which many felt were stronger. There were several anonymous letters to the newspapers, now known to be from Dr Johnson, criticising the elliptical arch as weak. A few weeks later an anonymous pamphlet appeared, under the name of Publicus, called *Observations on Bridge Building and the several Plans offered for the New Bridge*, which

The first Blackfriars Bridge in an image from a guidebook of 1817.

further fuelled the debate by criticising all the entries except Mylne's. Gwynn's bridge was a 'trifling gewgaw', Dance's old-fashioned and Smeaton's 'the weakest of all the designs'. Mylne's design, however, was 'superior for utility, strength, elegance, magnificence, and the ingenuity in its manner of construction'. Mylne almost certainly wrote the pamphlet himself or had a hand in its publication, but it seems to have had the desired effect. As well as having his design selected, he was appointed to supervise the construction, which was a great honour and responsibility for such a young and inexperienced architect.

There was, of course, the usual opposition to the scheme from the watermen, who would lose business, and they were compensated with a payment of £12,500. As the Bridge House Estates was rather short of money, it contributed only a small part of the expected cost of £160,000, apparently from the accumulated fines paid by men who had refused the post of Sheriff. The rest of the money had to be borrowed at 4 per cent interest.

Work began on 7 June 1760, when the first pile was driven in. The foundation stone was laid on 31 October, when the Lord Mayor, Sir Thomas Chitty, placed in it a set of coins and a tin plate that carried a eulogy in Latin to William Pitt, the Prime Minister, after whom the bridge was to be named. It is also thought that, before the time capsule was sealed, Mylne impulsively added one of his two prize medals at the last minute.

Like Labelye at Westminster Bridge, Mylne used caissons to build the piers but, to make them more stable, he first drove piles into the riverbed to support them. By 1764 the central arch was complete and, to celebrate the occasion, the Lord Mayor, along with Aldermen and Sheriffs of the City, were rowed through it in the state barge. Further progress, however, was slow, partly because of regular delays in the supply of stone, and in 1766 an extra £91,000 was needed to complete the work. Although still incomplete, in 1766 the bridge was opened to pedestrians, which helped to bring in some much-needed revenue, and in 1768 those on horseback were also allowed to use it. The bridge was fully opened on 19 November 1769, to general acclaim, but there was no opening ceremony. By the time the bridge was finished William Pitt was out of favour, and it was renamed Blackfriars Bridge, after the monastery that used to occupy the north bank at this point.

Mylne's original design was highly ornate, with bas-reliefs and statues of naval heroes, but these were dropped to keep the cost down. The bridge that was actually built was more restrained, but still very classical, and was much influenced by the work of Mylne's Italian teacher, Piranesi. It was built of Portland stone, which is a beautiful material, but rather soft, and parts of the structure, especially the cutwaters, can be seen in William Marlow's painting of around 1790 to have been damaged by ice or passing barges. The bridge had nine arches, the piers being decorated with pairs of Ionic columns, above which were elegant refuges for pedestrians. The total cost of the bridge, including the approaches, was £230,000. On the northern bank, this had included covering over the Fleet Ditch, which had become an open sewer by this time (the Fleet river still empties into the Thames via an outflow pipe visible today at low tide). Mylne had designed wide approaches on both sides of the river, including, on the south side, Surrey Street (now Blackfriars Road), which terminates

at St George's Circus, where the obelisk designed by Mylne, which shows distances to various London landmarks, can still be seen.

A highly ornate design by Mylne for his new bridge, which was not carried out.

The tolls, a halfpenny for pedestrians on weekdays, and a penny on Sundays, brought in a healthy income, but they were very unpopular with the public. During the Gordon Riots in 1780, the tollhouse was burnt down and the account books were destroyed. Although the original intention was for the tolls to be collected until the bridge was paid for, the weekday toll was discontinued in 1785, though the Sunday toll continued until 1811. From reports in *The Times*, it would appear that the rate of suicides and attempted suicides from the bridge increased substantially after it was freed from toll, though never reaching the levels at Waterloo Bridge.

Sadly, Mylne's bridge was to last for less than a hundred years, as the Portland stone was quickly eroded by the river and the pollution from the Fleet river, while the scour of the tidal Thames undermined the foundations. The increased flow of the river was caused by the changes to London Bridge, which no longer held back the power of the Thames. In 1791 *The Times* carried 'a very curious letter from Blackfriars Bridge to her Repairing Committee', in which the bridge complains that 'Your inattention to your duty has exposed me to the derision of every waterman… Indeed I am quite ashamed of my nakedness from top to bottom, in such a tattered condition is my clothing.' Repairs were carried out in 1793, when the damaged masonry was replaced by Aberdeen granite, a much harder stone, and one which was to be much used in building later bridges.

There had also been many complaints about the state of the roadway, which was always full of potholes, causing many accidents. In 1824 the road surface was macadamised, using a new invention consisting of small pieces of granite bound with gravel, offering better drainage. This method, invented by John Loudon McAdam, had already been used successfully on Westminster Bridge, and he supervised the

work himself. At the same time the steep gradients were levelled and the bridge approaches raised. Although the new road surface had its critics, traffic over the bridge increased, and business on the two adjacent bridges at Southwark and Waterloo, both still charging tolls, suffered as a result.

Despite these improvements, the bridge continued to deteriorate, and in 1832 a thorough survey was carried out by James Walker, the engineer who built Vauxhall Bridge. His report confirmed that extensive repairs were required and, under his supervision, work began in 1835. This included refacing much of the stonework with granite and strengthening the piers. The original columns were also replaced by granite ones, and the open balustrade was replaced by a plain parapet. The work took six years to carry out, as only one river pier could be repaired at a time so as to keep the river clear for navigation.

By the middle of 1850 it became clear that the repairs had been to no avail when one of the piers began to sink, and the bridge was closed for temporary repairs. Wooden centrings were installed to support the two affected arches, some of the stonework was removed from above them to lighten the bridge, and sections of the parapet were replaced in wood, which was given a coat of stone-coloured paint to blend in with the real stonework.

By now it had become clear that the bridge was beyond repair, and that there was little point in wasting more money in trying to maintain it. In 1853 the decision was made to replace the old bridge with a new structure, but no action was taken and the sad ruins of Mylne's once magnificent bridge were to remain in place for many more years. Two new major projects were to force the hand of the indecisive authorities. One was the plan for an embankment from Westminster Bridge to Blackfriars, which would reclaim about 130 feet of the river foreshore, changing the flow of water, which would further damage the weak structure of the bridge. The other was a new railway bridge that was to be built across the Thames just downstream of the road bridge for the London, Chatham & Dover Railway.

Twenty designs were sent from many eminent engineers and architects, including Thomas Page and Sir John Rennie. The initial recommendation in early 1862 was to accept Page's plan for a graceful iron bridge of three arches, but the decision as to how many arches the bridge should have was deferred for further discussion. As the new railway bridge had to be a level one, it would need to have more than three spans, and it was important that the two bridges, being so close to each other, had the same number of arches, to enable river traffic to pass through freely. There was, therefore, considerable antagonism between the City of London and the railway company, for whom any delay meant a loss of revenue.

Finally it was agreed that both bridges would have five arches, and the railway company's engineer, Joseph Cubitt, was commissioned to design both. In August 1863 work began on building a temporary bridge downstream of the old road bridge. It was a solid two-tier timber structure with three iron girder spans, the lower level carrying the carriage traffic and the upper one pedestrians. It was finished and tested by March the following year and it opened in June, when the work of pulling down Mylne's tumbledown old bridge was able to get under way.

On 20 July 1865, amid great ceremony, the foundation stone of the new bridge was laid by the Lord Mayor. In December the first stone of one of the piers was laid by William Hawtrey, chairman of the Bridge House Estates Work on the new bridge went relatively smoothly and quickly. Amazingly, only two workmen lost their lives during the construction, which was quite an achievement, as around forty had died during the building of Rennie's London Bridge. The foundations for the four massive piers were laid more than 30 feet below the riverbed, using wrought-iron caissons. On a layer of concrete, bricks were set in cement, the whole then encased in granite, some of it re-used from the old bridge. Work on three of the piers went without hitch, but there was a six-month delay in building the first pier on the northern side, as the soil was much looser, because of the effluent from the Fleet River, which flowed into the Thames at this point. For this reason the caissons had to be sunk to more than 50 feet below the riverbed before clay was reached. A further delay was caused by having to co-ordinate the construction of the northern approaches with the building of the new embankment and railway. The final cost of the bridge was about £320,000.

Queen Victoria graciously agreed to make one of her rare public appearances to open the bridge, and it had been hoped the ceremony could take place on 24 May 1869, the Queen's fiftieth birthday, but the bridge was not ready in time. The official opening took place on 6 November, when the Queen also opened the new Holborn Viaduct. Although it was claimed it would be a fairly simple ceremony, pavilions capable of seating four thousand notable persons were erected on both sides of the bridge. Vast crowds were expected to line the royal route to get a rare glimpse of the Queen, and the temporary bridge was closed to vehicles and pedestrians for the day in case it collapsed under the weight of sightseers. The Queen arrived at Paddington by train from Windsor and then drove in procession over Westminster Bridge and along the south side of the river to the bridge, where she was met by the Lord Mayor. After the formalities, she passed slowly over the bridge and up to Holborn Viaduct for the second opening of the day.

Cubitt's five-span iron bridge was very different in style from the first bridge, with decoration in what was called Venetian Gothic style. At 75 feet wide, it was twice as wide as the old bridge, and it also had a much shallower gradient. The central span was 185 feet wide, the two adjacent spans 175 feet and the two shore spans 155 feet. Each arch consisted of wrought-iron ribs, the visible outer ones having open lattice spandrels. Great care was taken over the details, such as the attractive cast-iron balustrade, whose columns have a variety of decorative capitals with little trefoil arches between them. On the end of each pier is a monumental column of polished red granite, 7 feet in diameter and nearly 12 feet high. Each column is made up of three blocks of granite from the island of Mull and was polished by the Scottish Granite Company at their works near Glasgow. The columns are capped with intricately carved capitals of Portland stone, sculpted by John Birnie Philip, and each one is different. The four facing upstream include plants and birds from the upper parts of the Thames, while the four on the downstream side show birds and seaweeds from the estuary. Resting on top of the columns are pulpit-like refuges for pedestrians, complete with hard stone seats, a reminder, it is sometimes claimed, of the work of the old monastery. When the bridge first opened, the ironwork was painted a bronze green colour, with some of the detailing in gold. In 1934 the bridge was repainted in two shades of brown, but today it is a rather more cheerful red and white.

An engraving from the Illustrated London News *showing the two-tier temporary bridge, built alongside Blackfriars Bridge before its replacement.*

At the four corners of the bridge were massive plinths intended to hold monumental bronze equestrian statues, though no action had been taken by the time the bridge opened. It was not until 1880 that the Bridge House Estates resurrected the project by setting up a competition. Submissions were requested and several sculptors sent in models, but none was found to be suitable. The biggest problem was in finding the right subject matter for the sculpture. The least controversial idea was for historical figures such as Alfred the Great and the Black Prince, but there were also proposals for such subjects as 'The Triumph of the City of London' and 'Activity Directing Indolence and Sloth to Progress'! After years of indecision, the scheme was dropped in 1886, and lamp standards were placed on the plinths instead. The scheme was briefly revived in 1902, when it was suggested that equestrian statues of Edward VII, Queen Alexandra and the Prince and Princess of Wales should adorn the bridge, but fortunately this was not carried out. The plinths on the south side of the bridge can still be seen, now converted into staircases leading down to the riverbank.

One statue that was erected on the bridge was that of Queen Victoria, though it has been moved on several occasions, when improvements have been made to the bridge approaches. The statue now stands, atop a red granite plinth, on a traffic island at the north end of the bridge she opened, looking up New Bridge Street towards Holborn Viaduct. It was made by Charles Bell Birch and was unveiled by the Duke of Cambridge on 21 July 1896. The statue was a gift to the City from Sir Alfred Seale Haslam but, as the City discovered later, it was not the only version of the sculpture. It was originally commissioned by the Maharana of Meywar, where it was erected in Udaipur in 1889 to celebrate the Queen's Golden Jubilee, and further copies had already been put up in Aberdeen and in Adelaide, Australia.

By the early years of the twentieth century, trams had become an increasingly popular form of transport, but there was great opposition to them operating in central London. The London County Council's proposal to run them over Blackfriars Bridge was delayed by resistance from the City of London, but the LCC won the support of Parliament, and the City finally agreed to the widening of Blackfriars Bridge to accommodate two lines of trams. Work began in 1907 to widen the bridge by 30 feet on the upstream side, to designs by Sir Benjamin Baker and Basil Mott. This involved digging new foundations to lengthen the piers and rounding off the junction on to the Embankment. The northern approaches to the bridge had long been considered a dangerous place for pedestrians, and this would be worsened by the regular passage of trams, so it was decided also to build a pair of intersecting pedestrian subways, which would be paid for by the LCC.

The widened bridge was officially opened on 14 September 1909. At 105 feet wide, it was the widest road bridge in London, and still is. The Lord Mayor was driven in his splendid gold coach from the Mansion House to a pavilion on the north side of the bridge. After the customary speeches, he declared the bridge open and drove the first tramcar across the bridge, to great cheers from the assembled crowds. The public tram services began that afternoon. It had been hoped that the subway would open at the same time, but there were delays because of the need to re-route the various pipes and sewers encountered. It was finally opened by the Lord Mayor on

A postcard view of the present Blackfriars Bridge shortly before it was widened. Behind it is the original railway bridge, of which only the piers now remain.

29 November and was to prove a great benefit to commuters, especially to those using the Underground and the trams. It was one of the first pedestrian subways built in London and is still in use today. The tram service ceased to operate in 1953, when the tracks were removed from the bridge.

During the 1960s a vehicular underpass was built under the north end of the bridge. During its construction, the remains of a first-century AD Roman ship were uncovered in the Thames mud, and Blackfriars Bridge was a perfect vantage point for interested spectators to watch the archaeologists working on the excavation. The boat still carried some of its cargo of ragstone, brought up from Kent for use as building material. Parts of the wooden ship were lifted from the mud and preserved at the Guildhall Museum. Some of the finds can now be seen in the Museum of

Blackfriars Bridge today, with St Paul's Cathedral and other City buildings forming a backdrop.

London's Roman Gallery, including a copper coin with the image of the goddess Fortuna, which, in a traditional Roman custom, had been placed under the mast to give the ship and its crew good luck.

The most dramatic event in the history of Blackfriars Bridge occurred on 18 June 1982, when the body of Roberto Calvi was found hanging from scaffolding underneath the northernmost arch of the bridge, his pockets filled with bricks and thousands of pounds in foreign currency. Calvi was the chairman of the Vatican's bank, the Banco Ambrosiano, which had recently been in difficulties, and he was referred to as 'God's Banker'. He had been involved in a number of financial scandals, and he was also a member of the notorious 'Propaganda Due', or P2, Masonic lodge, whose activities had been instrumental in bringing down the Italian government in 1981. Calvi had been found guilty in Italy of currency offences but had jumped bail to come to London on a false passport (which was found in his pocket) and had been staying secretly in Chelsea Cloisters. Why, then, was his body found so far from Chelsea? Members of P2 referred to themselves as *Frati neri*, or Black Friars, so it has been suggested that there was symbolism in the choice of the bridge. There were strong suspicions that Calvi had been murdered by members of the Mafia, but the inquest verdict in July was suicide. The Calvi family challenged the verdict and in March 1983 it was overturned in the High Court and a new inquest was ordered, which returned an open verdict. Some years later a Mafia informer alleged that Calvi had been killed by the Mafia and so, in 1998, Calvi's body was exhumed, and forensic tests suggested that he may indeed have been murdered. In 2005 five people, including a Mafia boss went on trial in Rome accused of his murder, but in 2007 they were acquitted as there was insufficient evidence to convict them. The mystery is therefore no nearer a solution.

There are a number of interesting things to look out for on and around the bridge. In the pedestrian underpass on the south side, the history of the road and railway bridges is illustrated on the tiled walls. On an island in the middle of the road on the south side is a dragon marking the boundary of the City of London. Although the borough and parish boundaries in London run down the centre of the Thames, the City's jurisdiction here includes all of the bridge, as it was built by the City. Alongside the bridge on the south side is the Doggett's Coat and Badge public house, which commemorates the annual river race competed for by apprentice watermen every July. The race starts, not at Blackfriars Bridge, but at London Bridge.

One of the upstream piers of Blackfriars Bridge, with its ornately carved capital depicting the wildlife of the Thames.

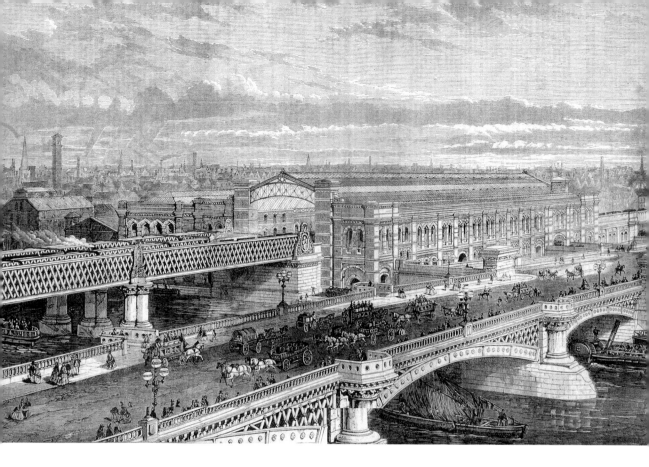

BLACKFRIARS RAILWAY BRIDGE

ETWEEN the road and rail bridges at Blackfriars is the somewhat surprising sight of rows of red columns stretching across the river. These are all that is left of the first railway bridge to be built here by the London, Chatham & Dover Railway. The LC&DR wanted to build an extension from its terminus near Beckenham across the Thames to link up with the Metropolitan Railway at Farringdon. In doing so, they would be the first company to serve the City from south of the river. They received authorisation from Parliament in 1860 and Joseph Cubitt was appointed to build the bridge. As the new bridge was to be very close to the Blackfriars road bridge, which was due to be rebuilt, there was a delay in agreeing the designs, and these delays were very costly to the railway company. In the end Cubitt was commissioned to build both bridges.

Work began in 1862. The bridge was to carry four lines of track and it had five spans of wrought-iron lattice girders. For each of the piers, three cast-iron cylinders were sunk into the river, faced with stone, filled with concrete, and finally covered in granite. On each one were placed four-shafted iron columns with ornate capitals, which were to support the superstructure. The abutments were built of brick and faced with Portland stone from old Westminster Bridge, which had been demolished

Engraving from the Illustrated London News *of the first Blackfriars Railway Bridge and the station on the south bank.*

130

in 1861. On the abutments the railway company's coat of arms was displayed on ornate cast-iron pylons, painted in bright colours to make a strong impression. Those at the south end can still be seen and are an impressive sight.

The bridge took less than two years to build, at a cost of £220,000, and was opened on 21 December 1864. A new station had been built on the south bank of the river, as well as another in Ludgate Hill. The line was connected up to the Metropolitan Railway in 1866, and the extension was later used by other railway companies. There was much criticism of the utilitarian design of most of the railway bridges over the Thames in London, but this one was considered to be well designed, especially when the columns were painted brown and the capitals gilded. The complaints were mostly because of the close proximity of the two bridges, which did not allow the much-admired new road bridge to be fully appreciated from all angles.

By the 1880s the traffic had increased so much that the bridge could not cope, and plans were made to widen Cubitt's bridge. This was not found to be a viable proposition, so a second railway bridge was built alongside the first one on the downstream side, carrying seven extra tracks. The bridge, known as the St Paul's Railway Bridge, was designed by Sir John Wolfe-Barry and Henry Marc Brunel (Isambard Kingdom Brunel's second son), and the foundation stone was laid in January 1884. The bridge has five wrought-iron arches and, because of the many criticisms of the earlier bridge, is rather more decorated, including masonry 'pulpits' above the piers. It originally had a Gothic-style cast-iron parapet, but this has now been replaced with a more functional one. The bridge was opened on 10 May 1886 and served the new St Paul's station on the north side of the river.

The two Blackfriars railway bridges. While the second one is still in use, all that remains of the first one are the piers.

In 1923 the railways were reorganised, and the new Southern Railway decided to concentrate its continental services at Waterloo and Victoria, so that from then on St Paul's station offered only local and suburban services. The station was renamed Blackfriars in 1937. In the 1950s there was a proposal to demolish both the station and the railway bridge, but instead the service to Holborn Viaduct was closed. In 1971 all services had to use the newer bridge and the superstructure of the old bridge was removed in 1985, leaving just the piers.

The Snow Hill tunnel, which had been opened in 1866 to carry the LC&DR's trains to Farringdon, had closed to passenger traffic in 1916, though it continued to carry goods trains until the late 1960s. In 1986, however, the track was relaid and the line was reopened to allow a new north–south service to operate, carrying passengers through London from Brighton to Luton and Bedford, serving both Gatwick and Luton Airports. The service opened in 1990 and has proved such a success that the lines between Blackfriars and London Bridge are now a serious bottleneck. To relieve the congestion, there are plans to upgrade the line, which will involve building a new Blackfriars station, with platforms right across the river on the railway bridge, allowing access from both sides of the river.

The colourful coat of arms of the London, Chatham and Dover Railway still stands on the south side of the old Blackfriars Railway Bridge.

MILLENNIUM BRIDGE

Following its dramatic opening and embarrassing closure in 2000, the Millennium Bridge has become one of London's best-known bridges and is now one of its most popular film locations. Less well-known is the fact that there had been plans for a road bridge at this spot 150 years earlier. The first proposal for a bridge here was put forward in 1853, and ten years later there were discussions about a pedestrian bridge at the same location. Nothing more was heard of the idea until 1909, when a more serious proposal was put forward to build a bridge that would relieve the congestion on London and Blackfriars Bridges and provide a new major route through central London. The cost, estimated at nearly £2 million, would be borne by the Bridge House Estates, though the London County Council was willing to contribute if the bridge could be built to carry trams, thus linking the systems north and south of the river. The debate over such a bridge, which was known as the St Paul's Bridge, was to continue for over twenty years before it was finally abandoned. The main concerns were about the quality of the bridge design, about its close proximity to St Paul's Cathedral and the potential damage a busy road would cause to its fabric. In 1911 the City succeeded in getting the legislation for the bridge through Parliament and managed to raise the finance, and a competition was held, attracting a number of grand monumental schemes. With the outbreak of the First

The Millennium Bridge, with St Paul's Cathedral in the background.

World War the plans had to be shelved, but in 1921 the project was resurrected, though less money was now available.

By now the future of the proposal was closely linked to the scheme for a new road bridge at Charing Cross. Most professional opinion was in favour of building a bridge at Charing Cross as a better way of relieving the congestion in central London, and the St Paul's Bridge fell out of favour, though the City continued to lobby for it. The matter was considered, as part of a wider overview of the subject, by the Royal Commission on Cross-River Traffic in London in 1926. In its report, the Commission recommended that the St Paul's Bridge scheme be abandoned, though even then the City would not drop the plan, and in 1928 it put forward a new proposal for a northern approach route further away from the cathedral. In 1931, partly owing to financial constraints, the scheme was finally dropped.

It was not until the 1990s that new plans for a bridge on this stretch of the Thames were put forward. The new bridge was the brainchild of David Bell, who worked for the Pearson media group, and who, as managing director of the *Financial Times*, had once worked in its offices overlooking the Thames by Southwark Bridge. In 1996 he approached the Royal Institute of British Architects about a proposal for a bridge and they suggested a competition to find a suitable design. As the first new bridge over the Thames in over one hundred years, there was great interest and there were 227 entries from all over the world. The winning design was from architects Foster & Partners, engineers Ove Arup and the sculptor Sir Anthony Caro. It was chosen because of its clean, simple lines, allowing it to blend in with the riverscape. It was a

Sir Albert Edward Richardson's grandiose design for the St Paul's Bridge, which was planned for a site close to the Millennium Bridge.

suspension bridge, but the cables supporting it would be to the side instead of above, as was traditional, allowing uninterrupted views up and down the river. Originally it was to be a horizontal bridge, but during the development process it was given its graceful curve, which was not only more elegant but also more practical, as it allowed for easier access at both ends. Because of its slim profile, Norman Foster described it as being by day 'a thin ribbon of steel and aluminium' and by night, when it was illuminated, a 'glowing blade of light'.

At this stage, there was no planning permission and it was still not clear where the bridge would be sited, especially in relation to St Paul's Cathedral and Giles Gilbert Scott's Bankside Power Station, then undergoing massive renovation as a new outpost of the Tate Gallery. While the design was being refined and tested, and funds were being raised, permission was sought from Southwark Council and the City of London. When this was received, along with a licence from the Port of London Authority, work could begin.

In early 1999 the Museum of London began a four-month archaeological excavation on both banks of the river, allowing them to examine the two historic waterfronts before the evidence was destroyed. Construction work began in April 1999, with the building of the coffer-dams to enable the piles to be driven into the bed of the river. The south abutment was the first to be completed, in September, when 1,000 cubic metres of concrete were poured in, followed by the north abutment, and finally the two piers. The huge V-shaped arms had to be installed on top of the piers before work could begin on the superstructure. A special hoist was erected to enable the cables to be put in place, and then the rest of the bridge was installed piece by piece. Different elements of the decking and balustrades had been made in factories all over Europe, including Poland, Finland and Germany. The parts were put together in the Thames estuary, brought up the river in sections, and the whole thing was assembled like a giant model kit. The pedestrian route down to the bridge from St Paul's was intended to have four pairs of markers designed by Sir Anthony Caro, but the authorities objected to them as being too obtrusive. All that remain are two large steel sculptures, known as the HSBC Gates, to mark the route by Queen Victoria Street, and two smaller pieces for people to sit on.

It had been hoped the bridge would open in early May 2000, at the same time as the opening of Tate Modern, but work fell behind schedule. However, on 9 May the Queen, accompanied by the Lord Mayor of the City of London and the Mayor of Southwark, walked on to the still incomplete bridge to dedicate it. On 8 June the lighting of the bridge was celebrated with a spectacular firework display and on Saturday 10 June it was officially opened to the public. The embarrassing events of that day were reported around the world and have given the bridge a name it will retain forever.

A sponsored charity walk had been organised to mark the opening, and soon after the walkers started to cross the bridge it began to sway slightly. When members of the public were allowed on at lunchtime, the numbers were far greater than expected, and the 'wobble' was much more pronounced, especially on the central and southern spans. The movement was so great that people had to hold on to the handrail to stay upright, and it was feared someone might fall over and be injured. The bridge was closed for engineers to make checks; when they pronounced the bridge safe, it was reopened, but with a limit on the numbers allowed on to it. Over the next couple of days the wobble was monitored and the bridge was closed on 12 June so that the engineers could find out what had gone wrong and look for a solution.

The engineers found that the problem was caused by the number of people using the bridge, not by any structural fault. All suspension bridges move, but, when a certain number of people walk on a bridge, the natural damping in the structure no longer works. In this case, when pedestrians felt the sideways movement they adjusted their steps to the bridge's motion, making the movement even greater, eventually resulting in the violent wobble experienced.

The solution was the installation of dampers, but this had to be done without affecting the appearance of the bridge. After tests were carried out, around ninety dampers, which act like a car's shock absorbers, were installed during 2001. Most of them were placed underneath the deck, where they are almost invisible. The most visible dampers are the diagonal ones on either side of the pier arms, but these were so well designed that they appear to be part of the bridge's original design.

At the end of January 2002 the Mayor of Southwark led two thousand volunteers over the bridge to test the repairs. The results were very positive, so the bridge finally reopened on 22 February. Although the bridge no longer wobbles, it will forever be known as the 'wobbly bridge'. Today it is busy at all times of the day, and tourists and Londoners alike use it, enjoying the views up and down the Thames without the noise and vibration of traffic or trains experienced on other bridges.

The whole project cost £23 million, £5 million of which was spent on installing the damping, and this was £7 million over budget. Over £7 million of the funds came from the Millennium Commission, a similar amount was contributed by the Bridge House Estates, and HSBC was the biggest corporate sponsor. The bridge is now maintained by the Bridge House Estates.

A view of the almost-permanently crowded Millennium Bridge from Tate Modern.

SOUTHWARK BRIDGE

BY the early nineteenth century London Bridge and the relatively new Blackfriars Bridge were both becoming congested and there were demands for a new bridge between them to relieve the pressure. As this was a fairly narrow part of the river, there was considerable opposition from the City of London and the Thames Conservators, as it was considered that a bridge there would be an impediment to river traffic. However, a Southwark Bridge Company was formed and it managed to obtain an Act of Parliament in 1811 allowing it to build a new bridge. John Rennie was appointed engineer and he designed a three-arched cast-iron bridge, which would allow the widest possible waterway. The central arch, at 240 feet, was the largest cast-iron span ever built. It was, however, only 43 feet wide, including two footpaths 7 feet wide.

Work began in 1814, which meant that Rennie was building two bridges concurrently, as work on his Waterloo Bridge had started in 1811. Timber coffer-dams were used to drive elm piles into the riverbed, and wooden rafts were placed on top. The foundation stone was laid in the south pier on 23 March 1815 by Admiral Lord Viscount Keith, attended by members of the Southwark Bridge Company committee, and a selection of current coins was placed underneath it. The inscription on the stone stated that 'the work was commenced at the glorious termination of the

Southwark Bridge as seen from Bankside 1819 by Rudolph Ackermann.

longest and most expensive war in which the nation has ever been engaged'. This was rather premature, as the Battle of Waterloo was several weeks away, but the inscription was obviously written when Napoleon was still imprisoned on Elba. The piers themselves were of granite from Peterhead, selected personally by Rennie's eldest son, John. The girders for the cast-iron arches were made by Walker's of Rotherham, and it is said that the work almost bankrupted the company. Rennie used the contractors Jolliffe & Banks, a company he had successfully worked with before and would use again, and as a result the bridge was built so efficiently that, instead of the five years stipulated in the contract, it was built in four.

The bridge was brilliantly illuminated for its low-key opening at midnight on 24 March 1819. The company had overspent its budget by nearly £200,000 and was unable to pay for anything more extravagant. Moreover, they tried to offer Rennie less money than he was due, but after he wrote to them he received his full fee, though only half the expenses he was owed.

Rennie's bridge is the 'iron bridge' that appears in Dickens' novels *Little Dorrit* and *Our Mutual Friend*. It is between London Bridge and Southwark Bridge that *Our Mutual Friend* opens, with Gaffer Hexham and Lizzie fishing bodies out of the Thames. Little Dorrit loves walking over the 'iron bridge' because it is quiet, and it is on the bridge that John Chivery proposes to her.

The bridge was an amazing engineering achievement and was much praised. Robert Stephenson was particularly fulsome, calling it 'unrivalled as regards its colossal proportions, its architectural effects and the general simplicity and massive character of its details'. Financially, however, it was never a great success, and the shareholders made little, if any, interest on their investment. The bridge's approaches were inadequate, as it was not on a through route, its roadway was too steep for horse-drawn vehicles and, being privately built, it was a toll bridge and could not hope to compete with either London Bridge or Blackfriars Bridge, which were both free. Most of the toll collected came from pedestrians, and after the opening in 1831 of Rennie's new London Bridge, the toll revenue fell by nearly half, and continued to fall after that. As early as 1840 there were demands, from traders on both sides of the river, for the bridge to be made toll-free. Meanwhile, the congestion on the two neighbouring bridges continued to increase, and in 1849 the Bridge House Estates offered to buy the bridge. The bridge company asked for £300,000, less than half the cost of construction, but the City still felt that the price was too high and no agreement was reached. It should perhaps be noted that this figure had previously been offered for the bridge by the North Kent Railway, who wanted to use it to take a railway over the river at this point, a plan turned down by the City.

Negotiations continued and in 1864 the City agreed to rent the bridge for an experimental six-month period. On 8 November, in a joint ceremony, the committees of the bridge company and the Bridge House Estates opened the bridge toll-free. After the tolls were dropped the user numbers increased significantly, including ten times as many pedestrians, who no longer had to pay the penny toll. The experiment was continued for a further twelve months, and in May 1866 the City finally bought the bridge for £215,000, and the hated tollbooths were taken down.

Jolliffe & Banks

Edward Banks (1770–1835) was a Yorkshireman of humble descent, who began his working life as a labourer in the construction industry, though his talent and determination saw him rise to the very top of the profession. Aged only twenty-one, he was the contractor for the Leeds & Liverpool Canal and he first worked with John Rennie in 1793 on the Lancaster and Ulverston canals. In 1803 he was in Surrey building the Croydon to Merstham extension of the Surrey Iron Railway, whose trucks were pulled by mules. One of the users of the railway was the quarry at Merstham, whose stone had been used in the rebuilding of London Bridge after the Great Fire of 1666. The owners of the quarry were the Jolliffe family, and Colonel Hylton Jolliffe MP went into partnership with Banks. In 1807 his place was taken by his brother, the **Reverend William Jolliffe** (1774–1835), and they were soon one of the most important contractors in the country, building canals, docks, lighthouses and bridges.

London's enclosed dock systems were developed during the early years of the nineteenth century, and Jolliffe & Banks, on the recommendation of Rennie, were involved in several of them, including the West India Dock and the London Docks. They were the contractors for all three of John Rennie's bridges in London and also worked on two of the bridges designed by his son, George Rennie, across the Serpentine in Hyde Park and over the Thames at Staines. They also worked with John Rennie on the naval dockyard at Sheerness and a scheme to drain vast areas of the Fens in Norfolk. In 1824 Jolliffe & Banks diversified by founding the General Steam Navigation Company, a highly successful business that for many years ran passenger and cargo services both on the Thames and across to the Continent.

The two men seem to have had a close personal

The monument to Sir Edward Banks in Chipstead Church in Surrey. All three of the bridges he built for Rennie feature on the memorial, with the bust of Banks himself sitting on an arch of London Bridge.

relationship as well as a good working partnership. Banks' second wife was the sister of his partner's wife, and one of Banks' daughters married Jolliffe's son.

Banks was knighted by George IV in 1822 for his work on Waterloo and Southwark Bridges, the first engineer to be so honoured. When he died he was buried in the churchyard of St Margaret's, Chipstead, Surrey, a spot he chose because he had fallen in love with the area when he was working on the Iron Railway. He was so proud of his work on the three Thames bridges that they all appear on his monument inside the church. His bust stands on a depiction of London Bridge, with Waterloo and Southwark on either side.

It soon became clear that, at only 42 feet wide, the bridge could not cope with the increase in traffic, and many suggestions were put forward to improve the approaches to it and lessen the steepness of the incline, especially on the northern side. The London County Council wanted to run a tram service over the reconstructed bridge, though this was not popular with the City. In 1912 the decision was finally taken to build a completely new bridge on the same site. It was designed by Basil Mott, with architectural detail provided by Sir Ernest George, and work began on its construction in 1913. Temporary steel bridges were erected on either side of the old bridge for pedestrians to use during the work, and they were also used to carry the cranes and gantries used in the construction. The foundation stone was laid on 20 November 1914 by W. Hayward Pitman, chairman of the Bridge House Estates. Instead of the three spans of the old bridge, the new one has five steel spans, so that the piers are aligned with the adjacent bridges, making river navigation safer. It is 55 feet wide, with 35 feet of roadway and two footpaths 10 feet wide. So that the same abutments could be used, the footpaths were cantilevered out in order to accommodate the extra width. The new bridge has 3 feet less headway than the old bridge, which gives it shallower gradients.

The granite piers had been completed by the time war broke out, so work was allowed to continue until 1917, when it had to stop because of the shortage of labour and the difficulty of obtaining the steel. Work resumed after the war was over, but, because of the high cost of building materials, some of Sir Ernest George's architectural details were not completed. There were to be tall piers at each end of the bridge topped by emblematic figures, but these now stop at the parapet. On the river side of the curious little refuges there were to be carved heads of tritons, but these were never added, and there is a strange empty shelf on each one.

The bridge was officially opened on 6 June 1921 by George V, accompanied by Queen Mary. There had been suggestions that the new bridge should be renamed as either the Victory Bridge or the King George Bridge, but the King requested that it retain its old name. The bridge cost £375,000 to build, all of the money coming from the funds of the Bridge House Estates.

Soon after the new bridge opened, the LCC again asked for permission to run a tram route over it, instead of stopping at the terminus on the south side of the bridge, and thus offering a more comfortable journey for thousands of City workers. This time the City gave its permission, probably because the bridge leads to a dead end, as they would not have allowed trams to drive through the City itself. On 14 July 1925, when the extension was officially opened, the Lord Mayor drove the first car over the bridge, and later the same day normal services began. The service terminated in the early 1950s, when trams were replaced by bus services.

In August 1972 Southwark Bridge was crowded with thousands of spectators watching the first tightrope walk across the Thames. Franz Burbach had failed in a similar attempt a year earlier, but this time he got across with no difficulties, though a twenty-five-year-old woman who decided on the spur of the moment to follow him was not so lucky. She tried to swing across by hand but fell into the Thames and had to be rescued.

In the early hours of 20 August 1989 one of the worst disasters on the Thames happened at Southwark Bridge. A 90-ton pleasure cruiser, the *Marchioness*, packed with young party-goers, was sailing downstream towards the bridge, when it was hit by a 2,000-ton dredger, *Bowbelle*, which was travelling in the same direction. The dredger ran right over the *Marchioness*, which sank in less than a minute. Fifty-one people, mostly young, died in the accident. There is a memorial to the victims in nearby Southwark Cathedral. Following the disaster, a number of improvements

The present Southwark Bridge.

were made to safety on the Thames, including the setting up of the first lifeboat service on the river in 2002.

On the north bank beside the bridge is Vintners' Hall, the home of the Vintners' Company, one of the twelve 'great' livery companies of the City. They share the ownership of swans on the Thames with the Dyers' Company and the Crown, and every year in July they take part in the traditional ceremony of Swan Upping, an annual census of swans, in which the cygnets are identified and marked as belonging to one of the three owners. The Swan Markers used to set off from Vintners' Wharf beside the bridge, but now they operate only between Eton and Abingdon.

It should be noted that, unlike London Bridge and Blackfriars Bridge, Southwark Bridge does not have silver dragons at its southern end to mark the City boundary. This is because the first bridge was built privately and not by the Bridge House Estates, so the boundary still runs across the centre of Southwark Bridge.

Today Southwark is still the Cinderella of London's bridges, with the least traffic. It has never had good approach roads, and it does not lead anywhere useful in either direction. As a member of the Metropolitan Board of Works said in 1856, it was 'like Punch's railway, it came from nowhere and went nowhere'. It is often said that if you find yourself on Southwark Bridge, you are probably lost, though it does provide a very useful dropping-off space for coaches taking visitors to the Globe Theatre.

CANNON STREET RAILWAY BRIDGE

IN 1861 the South Eastern Railway Company obtained an Act of Parliament to extend its line from London Bridge station across the Thames to a new station on Cannon Street, right in the heart of the City. Sir John Hawkshaw, as consulting engineer to the company, designed the station, the bridge and the viaducts leading up to it. The bridge was originally called the Alexandra Bridge after the Danish princess who married the Prince of Wales shortly before work began in 1863. The bridge and station opened on 1 September 1863. The bridge had five spans of girders resting on fluted Doric cast-iron cylinders, four to each pier, and decorated brackets formed a sort of cornice. The bridge was originally 89 feet wide and carried five tracks, and there was a footpath cantilevered out on each side, the downstream one for railway staff, and the upstream one for the public, who had to pay a halfpenny toll. In 1878 the bridge was freed from toll, but the company later closed the footpath to the public, and it has never been replaced. There was talk about a new footbridge being added to the bridge to celebrate Queen Elizabeth II's Golden Jubilee, but the idea seems to have been quietly shelved.

During 1889–92 the bridge was widened to 120 feet to accommodate an extra five tracks, when Francis Brady added two cylinders to each pier on the upstream side,

A photograph of Cannon Street Railway Bridge and station taken in about 1913.

at the same time removing the public footpath. In 1915–20 further strengthening work was carried out to carry heavier locomotives. In the late 1970s the bridge was rebuilt by British Rail, and the number of tracks was reduced again to five. During the work much of the decorative cast iron was removed and the Doric capitals were replaced by concrete.

When Cannon Street station was built, the foundations of a substantial first-century AD Roman building were found, and it is thought it may have been the palace of the provincial governor. In medieval and Tudor times it was the site of the Steelyard, the trading centre of merchants of the Hanseatic League from Germany. In September 2005 the Duke of Kent unveiled a plaque on the downstream wall of the station, overlooking the Thames Path, to commemorate this fact. The station, by Sir John Hawkshaw and Sir John Wolfe-Barry, had an arched iron and glass roof that was taller than the roof of St Pancras station. The only parts of the original station still standing are the distinctive pair of towers on either side of the platforms, and the side walls. The towers were built to house water tanks used to operate lifts. As part of the scheme there was a hotel on Cannon Street, designed by E. M. Barry in the Italianate style, but this was replaced in the 1960s with an office block by the notorious architect John Poulson, who was later jailed for corruption and bribery. In the 1980s the station roof was replaced by another office block, whose piles were driven through the station platforms. In 2007 it was announced that the railway and Underground stations, as well as the offices above are to be refurbished, though the station will continue to operate during the redevelopment.

Cannon Street Railway Bridge today, minus what little decoration it originally had.

ES nouuelles dalbyon

Il vous en plaist escoute

on frere z mon copaign

Aachez qua mon retou

Ay este sera la mer

LONDON BRIDGE

THERE has been a bridge on or near the site of the present London Bridge for nearly two thousand years. The first bridge was built by the Romans soon after their invasion of AD 43, at a point about 200 feet east of the modern bridge. We do not know exactly when the first bridge was built, but *Londinium* was an important city at the centre of a network of roads, so some sort of river crossing would have been needed. Archaeological evidence suggests that there were three bridges, the first being a wooden bridge erected possibly as early as AD 50, the last a more permanent structure probably in place by the end of the first century. This last one probably had stone abutments and brick piers, with a wooden superstructure, and it may later have had a drawbridge added, to allow ships to sail through. There may also have been a temple or shrine on the bridge, as many coins and small figurines have been found in the Thames near the site, presumably thrown into the river as votive offerings. After the Romans withdrew their army from Britain in AD 410, *Londinium* became a deserted city, so it is likely that by then the bridge had been allowed to decay, as it would have been very costly to keep it in good repair and there would have been little point in maintaining it.

After the departure of the Romans, various Germanic settlers arrived in Britain, and the Saxons settled in what they called *Lundenwic* to the west of the Roman city, though they took shelter from Viking invasions within the old walls, and King Alfred rebuilt the city as a fortress in the ninth century. As the new port was upstream of the old bridge, the bridge may not yet have been rebuilt, and the first documentary evidence of a new bridge dates from around AD 1000. As the eleventh-century port developed both above and below the bridge, it is assumed that the Saxon bridge also had a drawbridge to allow ships through. Between 1000 and the construction of the stone bridge, the timber bridge may have been rebuilt as many as five times.

As well as being a crossing point, the bridge also provided an extra line of defence for the city, stopping enemy ships from getting upstream of it, and preventing attackers from reaching the city by land. It played a dramatic part in the violent events of the early eleventh century, when London changed hands several times during the power struggle between the Saxons and the Vikings. The best-known tale relates to the attempt by the Saxon king Ethelred the Unready to recapture London from Cnut in 1014. He enlisted the help of the Norwegian King, Olaf, whose ships, fortified with canopies to protect the crew, sailed up to the bridge, attached grappling irons to it and sailed away, destroying or badly damaging it. This was the inspiration for the Norse poem from the *Olaf Sagas*, whose first verse is:

London Bridge is broken down,
Gold is won, and bright renown.
Shields resounding,
War-horns sounding,
Hildur shouting in the din!
Arrows singing,
Mailcoats ringing,
Odin makes our Olaf win!

OPPOSITE:
The earliest representation of the medieval London Bridge, seen here in the background of an image from a book of poems by Charles, Duke of Orleans published in about 1500. © British Library Board.

The poem is better known from the familiar nursery rhyme 'London Bridge is falling down', which first appeared in the seventeenth century. Olaf became a popular saint in England, and there were once three churches dedicated to him in London, including one at the southern end of London Bridge, which was replaced in 1931 by an office block called St Olaf's House. In 1016 Cnut returned to reclaim his throne and, as he was unable to take the bridge, he dug a channel round the south end of it and had his ships dragged round to the upstream side so that he could surround the city. After the Norman invasion of 1066, William of Normandy needed to take London to secure his power, but when he arrived at the southern end of it he found it well defended, and he had to take his army upstream, where he crossed the Thames and marched on London from the west.

Wooden bridges constantly required attention, as the wood decayed and needed replacement, and there was the constant risk of damage by floods or other natural disasters. The bridge had to be rebuilt after a storm severely damaged it in 1097, and again in around 1136 after it was badly burnt in a fire that destroyed most of the port. By the late twelfth century London was a prosperous community, making its money from the export of wool and cloth, so it was decided to replace the old wooden bridge with a more permanent stone structure, which would be much more expensive to build, but cheaper to maintain. This was a time when massive castles and cathedrals were being built, so there was plenty of experience available for such a major construction as the new bridge. The building of bridges in the Middle Ages was considered a work of piety, and the Church was often involved in their construction. London's new stone bridge was built under the guidance of Peter de Colechurch, priest of St Mary Colechurch, who had carried out the last rebuilding of the wooden bridge. Although the start of the construction is not recorded, it is thought that it was begun in 1176 and lasted over thirty years, being completed in 1209, four years after Peter's death. It is quite likely that the old timber bridge was retained during at least some of its construction. It has been said that the bridge was built on woolpacks, as Henry II imposed a tax on wool to fund its construction, though further funds were supplied by the Archbishop of Canterbury and the Papal Legate.

The bridge was about 906 feet long and 20 feet wide, and it had nineteen irregularly spaced piers, each sitting on large platforms or cutwaters, usually referred to as 'starlings'. There were twenty arches, varying in width from 15 to 34 feet, plus a drawbridge towards the Southwark end. The variation in the width of the arches has been much commented on and may have been due to the difficulty in finding firm ground to drive in the piles. Building the bridge was a massive undertaking, and one that could be highly dangerous, and as many as 150 men may have died during its construction. As there was no stone available locally, it had to be brought in from elsewhere, which added to the cost. The main stone used was Kentish ragstone, Purbeck stone from Dorset and Reigate stone from Surrey. The Thames, much wider then than it is today, is tidal, so that much of the work had to be carried out at low tide, and during the winter months the work could be damaged by floods and ice. The method of building the piers is known to us because detailed plans were made when the bridge was being demolished in the nineteenth century. An oval of short piles was driven in first, using a man-powered pile-driver balanced on two boats. This was then filled with rubble, so that they could build a bigger pile-driver on top of it. Using this, they built the starling, consisting of protective rows of longer piles round the outside, filling the gap with more rubble. It was on this platform that the stone piers were built, each block being made secure with an iron clamp and the joints sealed with pitch. To construct the arches, temporary wooden frames, or centrings, were built to support the work until the arch was finished.

At the southern end of the bridge were two fortified towers, the Stonegate and the Drawbridge Gate, which defended the city from attack from the south. There may well have been domestic houses on the bridge from the very beginning, as their rents were needed to help pay for the bridge's upkeep, and building space within the city's protective walls was at a premium. There were shops and businesses of all sorts along both sides of the roadway, including several inns, and the bridge would have looked just like any other busy city street. Indeed, because the houses were so tightly packed together, some visitors to London in later centuries claimed that they had found their way on to the bridge without realising it. Over one hundred inhabited bridges were built in Europe in the Middle Ages, but London Bridge was by far the longest and it was considered to be one of the wonders of the medieval world.

The first building to go up was a chapel, which was built on the downstream side of the largest island near the centre of the bridge, and it was here that Peter de Colechurch was buried. It was 60 feet high and had two rooms, the upper one at road level and the undercroft in the pier itself, with separate access from the river at low tide for sailors and watermen. The chapel was dedicated to St Thomas the Martyr, a popular London-born saint. Thomas Becket, when Archbishop of Canterbury, had been murdered in his cathedral in 1170 and was canonised in 1173, only three years before work on the bridge started. It is possible that the chapel was the starting and finishing point for pilgrimages to Canterbury, and many of the pilgrim badges found in the Thames near the bridge feature St Thomas, probably thrown into the river to give thanks for a safe return. The chapel at first had two priests and four clerks, so it was clearly considered to be important, and in the early years they were probably responsible for looking after the bridge's revenues. In the late fourteenth century the chapel was rebuilt in the Perpendicular style, but everything changed with the Dissolution of the Monasteries, as Henry VIII was particularly hostile to the cult of St Thomas. The dedication of the chapel was changed to St Thomas the Apostle in order to save it, but around 1550 it was deconsecrated and converted into a house. In 1553 it was occupied by a grocer, and later the building was altered beyond all recognition.

The bridge needed constant maintenance, owing both to damage and to normal wear and tear. The drawbridge had to be replaced several times and the starlings were in permanent need of repair, which was dangerous work that could be carried out only at low tide. All this was expensive and was paid for by charging rent on houses on the bridge, and by a toll levied on merchant vessels passing through the drawbridge. From 1281 a toll of a farthing was charged on pedestrians crossing the bridge, and horsemen were charged a penny. The bridge also relied on donations and bequests from Londoners, both rich and poor, some of which were in the form

Detail from a mid-
seventeenth century
Dutch painting of
London from Southwark.
Note the heads displayed
on the Stonegate.

of property. It was seen as a religious duty to support the work of repairing the great bridge, and many of the donors stated that the gift was 'to God and the Bridge'.

In 1212, when the bridge was barely three years old, it suffered the first of many fires. On this occasion there were fires at both ends of the bridge, trapping people in the centre of it. When ships pulled alongside to rescue them, such was the confusion that, according to John Stow's report in *A Survey of London*, about three thousand people died, though this may have been an exaggeration.

In 1282 part of the bridge actually did fall down. In 1249 Henry III had taken control of the bridge's revenues and in 1263 passed it on to his wife, the unpopular Eleanor of Provence. Because of her mismanagement of the funds, five arches of the bridge collapsed during the particularly severe winter of 1282–3 and the queen quickly gave up her responsibility for the bridge. The citizens of London, including the Mayor, paid for a temporary bridge to be built, so long as Parliament paid for the rebuilding of the bridge itself. In 1284 the Bridge House Estates were formed to look after the bridge, and they have cared for London Bridge ever since. More serious damage was caused by ice in 1437, when the Stonegate and two adjacent arches collapsed, thus causing disruption to the supply of essentials to the capital. A temporary bridge was quickly installed so that business could resume, and repairs were carried out. When the work was completed, the whole bridge was thoroughly inspected and rebuilt, piece by piece.

The Bridge House Estates occupied premises, known as Bridge House, at the southern end of the bridge, housing its administrative offices and a warehouse where they stored materials such as timber and masonry needed to carry out repairs to the bridge. As the operation needed large numbers of staff, including masons, carpenters and administrators, there was also a garden, where fruit and vegetables were grown to feed them, and also to entertain the Lord Mayor on his annual visit to audit the accounts. In 1831 the property was sold off to be redeveloped. The organisation, which is part of the City of London, is now a charity and has accumulated so much wealth over the years that its statutes have been amended to allow it to finance many good causes.

Because of the narrow gaps between the piers and the strong tide flowing between them, there was often a difference of up to 5 feet in the river level on either side of the bridge, so that passing through it was highly dangerous, and was referred to as 'shooting the bridge'. It has been calculated that at half tide, when the starlings were uncovered, the waterway would have been reduced to about 245 feet, less than a third of the length of the bridge. Later, when waterwheels blocked several arches, it would have been much less. Many boats overturned going through the arches, and many watermen and their passengers perished in the attempt. In 1429 the Duke of Norfolk nearly drowned when his barge hit one of the starlings and overturned. Several of his crew did drown, but he managed to climb on to one of the starlings and was rescued. Most people, including Cardinal Wolsey, got off at the bridge and walked or rode round it to pick up another boat, but Henry VIII regularly went through it. In his diaries, Samuel Pepys describes going through the bridge on several occasions, though more than once he had to get out and walk through on the starling. There was a popular saying that 'London Bridge was made for wise men to go over and fools to go under'.

It is not surprising that people often fell off the bridge, and they were usually swept away and drowned. One who was more fortunate was Anne, the daughter of William Hewett, a cloth worker who lived on the bridge. When she fell into the river from an upper storey in 1536, Hewett's apprentice, Edward Osborne, dived in and saved her. The story has a fairy-tale ending too, as Osborne later married her, and both men later became Lord Mayors of London. Hewett's portrait is on display in the Museum of London.

Tolls were charged on goods going over or through the bridge. Merchant ships could go through the drawbridge arch into the upper harbour of the port only when the tide was right, and the same applied to departing vessels. This meant that the bridge was opened to allow all the vessels to go through together, and movement over the bridge could be disrupted for an hour or so twice a day. The number of ship movements varied widely, depending on the time of the year and the state of the weather, so those crossing the bridge sometimes had a long wait to continue their journey, but there were several inns and taverns on or near the bridge to help people pass the time if they did not want to watch the ships passing through it.

The bridge had two quite different faces. The view from the bank or the river, with its great variety of buildings of different shapes and heights, was very picturesque, but these were the backs of the buildings, which in a city street would not normally be on public view, so no trouble was taken in making them look attractive. The façades overlooking the main roadway would have been very different, with much carved and painted decoration, like any other London street of the time. The bridge itself was only 20 feet wide, so that many of the buildings were cantilevered out over the river. Both sides of the roadway were thickly lined with shops, and it must have seemed much like any other shopping street in London. It would also have been very crowded, and extremely noisy, with the constant traffic both over and under it, and the shopkeepers and hawkers competing with each other to sell their wares. There must have been a fair amount of crime on the bridge too, especially thieves and pickpockets. As well as a set of stocks, there was also a 'cage' on the bridge, in which offenders could be exhibited to public ridicule.

The profile of the bridge changed greatly over the years as the buildings grew taller to create more living and working space, and by the sixteenth century some were four or five storeys high, with rooms built across the central roadway to create even more space. With buildings being regularly rebuilt, the style of architecture changed too, so that by the eighteenth century the bridge looked very different. The traders paid a high rent for their properties, but there was plenty of passing trade, so they must have done good business. However, the sanitation was fairly basic. As is clearly seen in many of the early depictions of the bridge, the privies were wooden shacks attached to the outside of the buildings, emptying straight into the Thames, which was very functional for the user, but less pleasant for those passing under the bridge. There was also a public privy on the bridge, which, according to Stow, fell into the river in 1481, killing five of its occupants.

Despite the defences on the bridge, some attackers got through. When Simon de Montfort tried to enter the city in 1264, the Lord Mayor closed the drawbridge and locked the gate, throwing the key into the river, but de Montfort was helped by some supporters, who broke down the gates to let him in. During the Peasants' Revolt of 1381 the bridge was again closed against the rebels, but it was opened when Wat Tyler threatened to burn down the houses at the southern end. In the 1450 rebellion Jack Cade and his followers threatened to set fire to the bridge, and the drawbridge was opened for them to cross. Later there was a fierce battle on the bridge that lasted all night but brought an end to the uprising. The bridge defended the city more successfully during Thomas Wyatt's rebellion in 1554, when he was forced to take his troops upstream to cross the river at Kingston.

From the early fourteenth century, heads of traitors were stuck on poles on the top of the Drawbridge Gate, as a warning to all those arriving in London from the south. To make the heads last longer, they were parboiled and then preserved in tar. Probably the first person to suffer this indignity was William Wallace, the Scottish warrior, who was hanged, drawn and quartered at Smithfield in 1305. Many famous and infamous heads were displayed here, including those of the rebels Wat Tyler and Jack Cade. During Henry VIII's reign, the heads of many of his political enemies were displayed on the bridge, most notably that of Sir Thomas More, who refused to acknowledge the king as head of the Church and was executed at Tower Hill. Before More's head was thrown in the river to make room for a new occupant, his daughter, Margaret Roper, is said to have bought the head and had it buried in the Roper vault at St Dunstan's Church in Canterbury. An alternative, but less likely, version, related by John Aubrey, has the head falling into her lap as she passed under the bridge. The head of Bishop Fisher was also displayed here, but after two weeks, instead of rotting, it was seen to be looking better every day and was attracting sightseers, so it was thrown into the Thames. After Nonesuch House replaced the Drawbridge Gate in 1577, traitors' heads were displayed on the Stonegate, and in 1592 a German visitor to London claimed to have seen over thirty heads on display there. After the return of Charles II in 1660, the heads of the regicides were added to the bridge's collection, but the grisly tradition was discontinued in 1678.

As the only entrance to London from the south, the bridge was often the scene of royal pageantry. In 1357 the Black Prince crossed it on his return from his victory at Poitiers, bringing with him the captured French king. In 1390 a jousting match was held on the bridge in the presence of Richard II, between an English knight and a Scottish opponent, the Scotsman winning. When Richard II arrived with his new French bride, Isabella, in 1396, huge crowds thronged the bridge to see her, and in the crush nine people were killed. On three occasions connected with the short life of Henry V the bridge was magnificently decorated for important events. In 1415 it welcomed him home after his famous victory at Agincourt, and again in 1421 when he brought back his French bride, Catherine. After his death in 1422 at Vincennes, his body was accompanied over the bridge by an impressive retinue of noblemen, bishops and soldiers, along with three hundred torch-bearers. During the Tudor period the bridge welcomed many important visitors, including Catherine of Aragon in 1501, on her way to marry Prince Arthur, and, in 1522, Emperor Charles V on a diplomatic visit. In 1660 Charles II crossed the bridge in a magnificent procession to claim his throne, accompanied by hundreds of soldiers and musicians.

In 1581 Pieter Morice, a Dutch engineer, was granted a five-hundred-year-lease to supply water to the city from a waterwheel in the first arch of the bridge. He had earlier demonstrated the capabilities of the new machinery by sending a jet of water over the steeple of St Magnus' Church. The operation was so successful that he was soon offered the lease of the second arch as well. Both wheels were destroyed in the Great Fire of 1666, thus hampering attempts to put out the fire, but they were rebuilt soon afterwards. In 1701 the concern was sold to a goldsmith by the name of Richard Soame, and by 1761 four arches were in use. One of these wheels supplied water to Southwark via pipes over the bridge, but later a new wheel was installed for the purpose under the second arch at the southern end. In the early nineteenth century, the company's heyday, it was supplying ten thousand customers with 4 million gallons of water a day, but in 1822 the operation was forced to close, as the wheels were considered to be a hazard to navigation. Although the original lease was for five hundred years, no new wheels were added to Rennie's new bridge as the water flow was much reduced, and the City refused to allow waterwheels inside the arches. The lease does not expire until 2082 and Thames Water still pays dividends to a number of shareholders.

Old London Bridge *by Samuel Scott, painted shortly before the buildings were removed.*

As the narrow openings in the bridge acted as a barrier, slowing down the tidal flow, the Thames often iced up, and ice floes caused regular damage to the bridge. In severe winters the river was completely iced over upstream of the bridge, and frost fairs were held on the river, with all sorts of food stalls setting up shop, and entertainments such as skating and bull-baiting taking place. Printing presses were set up, where one could buy a souvenir ticket with one's name on – the Museum of London has a ticket issued to Charles II. The first frost fair took place in 1607, and the last one was in 1814. By then the bridge had been given a wider central arch, which allowed the river to flow faster, so it no longer iced up as completely as before.

One of the biggest changes to the look of the bridge came in 1577, when the Drawbridge Gate, which was in a poor state, was demolished and replaced by Nonesuch House, so-called because there was no other like it. It was a highly ornate half-timbered building, with turrets at each corner, each one topped by a cupola and a gilded weathervane. Like many Elizabethan houses, there were so many windows that the walls seemed to be all glass, and it was covered in intricately carved woodwork and colourful decoration. No nails were used in its construction, and it was made in sections in Holland before being shipped across the Channel and put together rather like a modern flatpack.

In 1633 forty-two houses at the north end of the bridge were destroyed by a fire that had started in a house near St Magnus' Church when a maidservant carelessly left a tub of hot ashes under the stairs. In 1645 new, more modern buildings were erected over the northern part of the affected area, leaving a gap that would save the bridge from destruction only a few years later. In the Great Fire of 1666 the new buildings were destroyed as well as St Magnus' Church, though the bridge itself survived more or less intact, the main casualty being the waterworks at the north end. More seriously, the wreckage blocked the roadway, preventing the citizens from escaping over the bridge. The destroyed houses were rebuilt in 1683, according to the new strict guidelines for new houses in London after the fire, and the houses at the southern end of the bridge were later rebuilt in the same style, so beginning the change in the appearance of the bridge. (In 1640 a wealthy parishioner of St Magnus left money in her will for a sermon to be preached every year to thank God for preserving the church in the 1633 fire. Unsurprisingly, the custom was discontinued after 1666 but it has recently been revived.)

The carriageway of the bridge had been only 12 to 15 feet wide, barely enough for two vehicles to pass each other. As there were no pavements, it must have been very dangerous for pedestrians crossing the bridge, and they often found it safer to walk behind a vehicle. When the houses at the northern end were rebuilt following the fires of 1633 and 1666, they overhung the river even more than before, allowing the roadway to be widened, and later the whole roadway was widened as all the houses were replaced. To be able to widen the carriageway, the houses were built out on to the piers, hiding the arches from view, making the bridge look less attractive than before. When the Stonegate was rebuilt in 1728, its archway was widened to help keep the traffic moving. From 1722 tolls were charged on vehicles crossing the bridge, and three people were employed to make sure that they drove across the bridge on the left, the first time a 'keep left' rule, which we now take for granted, was enforced in England. In 1749, before Westminster Bridge had been completed, so many people wanted to attend the dress rehearsal of Handel's *Music for the Royal Fireworks* at Vauxhall Gardens that there was a three-hour traffic jam on London Bridge.

Old London Bridge, a watercolour by J. M. W. Turner, from about 1794, showing the eighteenth-century balustrade and one of the stone refuges.

By the eighteenth century the bridge had begun to look rather sad and many of its wealthier occupants had left. When Westminster Bridge opened in 1750, it was highly praised as both elegant and modern, prompting the City authorities to consider rebuilding London Bridge, but financial prudence led them to improve it instead. In 1736 Nicholas Hawksmoor had put forward a plan to replace the four central spans with two larger ones, but it was not until 1756 that it was decided to carry out improvements to the bridge. The radical modifications were the work of George Dance and Robert Taylor from 1757 to 1762. It involved demolishing all the buildings, widening the bridge by 26 feet out over the starlings, and removing the middle pier to create a wider central arch to improve river navigation. The whole bridge was refaced in Portland stone and given a balustrade, and stone alcoves were added over the ends of the piers, fourteen of them with domes, rather like those on Westminster Bridge. It was also decreed that the lighting should be improved, and lamps were kept burning from sunset until sunrise. While the work was being carried out, a temporary wooden bridge was built on the starlings on the western side of the bridge, though it had to be replaced after it burnt down in 1758, possibly an act of arson. Unsurprisingly, the faster flow of water through the wider central arch began to undermine the starlings, and stone from the demolished City gates was placed under the arch to prevent further scouring. When the Stonegate was demolished in 1760, the George II coat of arms over the arch, added when the gate was rebuilt in 1728, was bought and put up on a tavern in Axe Yard off Borough High Street, with the date and king changed to 1760 and George III. Appropriately, the stone sign now adorns the King's Arms public house on the same site, in what is now Newcomen Street. In 1763 arches were cut through the base of the tower of the Church of St Magnus the Martyr for pedestrians using the wider bridge. In 1782 the tolls were finally scrapped.

As London grew, new bridges were built to carry the increasing road traffic, but London Bridge continued to be congested, and the bridge itself began to show its age, so that there were regular calls for the 'Gothic nuisance', as one writer to *The Times* referred to it, to be replaced. In 1799 a competition was held for designs for a replacement bridge. The most original idea came from Thomas Telford, a leading force in the move towards the use of iron instead of stone. His plan was for a massive single-span cast-iron bridge 600 feet wide, but, although it gave ample headway for ships to pass under it, the curve of the arch meant the bridge would have needed long approach ramps, making the costs prohibitive, as it would have required the purchase of much privately owned riverside land. The design put forward by George Dance the Younger was much more classical, though equally impressive. It consisted of two bridges, with vast piazzas between them on each bank, one with an obelisk at its centre, and the other with Wren's Monument relocated to it. Each bridge had a drawbridge at its centre, so that traffic could use one bridge while ships passed through the other. As with Telford's design, this one was much liked, but it would have proved too expensive, again because of the need to buy up so much property along the riverbank.

Discussions continued for another twenty years as to whether the old bridge could be repaired or whether the money should be spent on a new structure. There were many complaints about the dangerous state of the bridge, especially after it was damaged during the severe winter of 1813–14, when the last frost fair was held. A decision was made in 1822, following debate in both the Court of Common Council and in Parliament, to recommend the construction of a new bridge, and the Act was passed in 1823. John Rennie, the architect of Waterloo and Southwark Bridges, had put forward a proposal for the new bridge in March 1821, but he died later that year. In 1823 a competition was held and more than fifty designs were submitted for the consideration of a panel including John Nash and Sir John Soane. The winner was William Fowler, but Parliament was not happy with the decision and opted for Rennie's design instead. His son, also called John, took on the responsibility of the bridge's construction, aided by his brother, George.

One of the eighteenth-century stone refuges from old London Bridge, now in the grounds of Guy's Hospital.

It was decided to build the bridge on a new alignment about 100 feet upstream of the old bridge, so that people could still cross over the old bridge while the new one was being built. The new alignment meant that new approaches had to be built, and there were prolonged discussions and negotiations in Parliament and the City on the matter. On the Southwark side, Borough High Street was widened, opening up views of St Saviour's Church (now Southwark Cathedral), but the Lady Chapel was threatened with demolition and only a determined fight by the church and its supporters saved it. On the northern side, many important buildings had to be demolished, including Wren's Church of St Michael, Crooked Lane, the old

Boar's Head tavern in Eastcheap (where Prince Hal and Falstaff caroused in Shakespeare's *Henry IV*) and Fishmongers' Hall. Compensation paid out to the landowners on both sides of the river added greatly to the cost of the new bridge.

The work of driving in the piles began in 1824 and in June 1825, with much ceremony, the first stone was laid by the Lord Mayor in a coffer-dam, which was accessed by a flight of steps from the old bridge. The bridge took over seven years to build, and forty lives were lost during its construction. In the end it cost nearly £2.5 million to build, including the cost of building the approaches, and a considerable amount of this was provided by a tax on coal. The new bridge was 56 feet wide and 1,005 feet long; it had five elliptical arches made of granite from Scotland and Devon, the central span being 152 feet wide. On both sides at each end were wide stairs leading down to the river, which served as piers for the steamboats that brought thousands of workers into the City each day, and for the pleasure boats that carried large numbers of people on day trips to Margate and Gravesend. During the building work, the river became very constricted and there were a number of accidents, some of them fatal, so two arches at each end of the old bridge were made into larger openings to allow river craft an easier passage.

Such a major new construction deserved a spectacular opening, and this is exactly what it received. The bridge was opened on 1 August 1831 by William IV and Queen Adelaide in a magnificent ceremony, which was captured on canvas by the artist Clarkson Stanfield, in a painting now in the Guildhall Art Gallery. The royal party drove from Buckingham Palace to Somerset House, where they boarded the Royal Barge, and were conveyed to the City in a procession of barges reminiscent of a scene from one of Canaletto's paintings. More decorated barges lined the riverbanks, including those of the City livery companies, all filled with spectators, and the quays and bridges were also packed with curious onlookers. The King and Queen were met at the steps of the bridge by the Lord Mayor, the Aldermen and members of the Bridge Committee, all dressed in their robes and uniforms. The Lord Mayor handed the City sword to the King, who returned it to him, in a traditional ceremony that still takes place when the monarch visits the City. The parties then walked across the bridge to the Southwark side to open it officially. There they were entertained by a balloon ascent by Charles Green before returning to the Royal Tent, which had been erected at the City end, for a banquet.

The whole bridge was decorated with flags of all nations, and the tables for the guests stretched halfway across the bridge. After the banquet there were toasts, but, somewhat unusually, no speeches. The royal party returned by river, accompanied by other boats, including the Lord Mayor in his barge, as far as Somerset House, and thence by carriage to Buckingham Palace. At 9 p.m. the barriers were removed and the public were allowed on to the bridge for the first time. The following day over 200,000 people crossed over it, but from the City side only, as the crowds were too great to allow people to cross in both directions. John Rennie junior was knighted for his work on the bridge, an honour his father was offered but had refused.

Now that the new bridge was open, the old bridge could be demolished, a task that took nearly two years. Concerns were voiced by such eminent engineers as John Smeaton and Thomas Telford that its removal would affect the tidal flow of the river so much that sluice gates would be required on the new London Bridge, and probably Westminster Bridge as well, to ensure that there would be enough water at low tide for ships to navigate the river. The tidal flow was, indeed, changed by the demolition of the bridge, but its effects were felt much further upriver, as explained in the chapter on Richmond Lock.

View of the old and new London bridges in 1830 by Edward William Cooke, showing the old bridge still crowded while work is carried out on the new one.

John Rennie (1761–1821)

John Rennie was one of the finest and most versatile engineers of his time. The youngest of nine children of a Scottish farmer and brewer, he was a precocious student, working, aged only twelve, for a local millwright to learn about mechanics. At the age of eighteen, he set up in business on his own as a millwright, while continuing his studies at Edinburgh University. He later went on a study tour of England and was introduced to James Watt in Birmingham. The following year Watt offered him a job installing the machinery at the Albion Mills, an innovative flour mill on the south side of Blackfriars Bridge in London. The mill opened in 1786 but burnt down five years later, by which time Rennie had made his reputation. He soon began to supply machines to businesses in Europe and Britain, including new machinery for the Royal Mint. By 1810 his business had grown so much that he built a new factory on the site of the old mill. In 1791 he moved to a house in Stamford Street, a short distance from the factory, where he lived until his death.

In 1790 he was appointed surveyor for the Kennet & Avon Canal and so began his involvement in civil engineering, especially related to water, such as harbour improvements and drainage schemes. In London he played an important part in the development of the new enclosed docks, working on the London, East India and West India Docks. He also designed the mile-long breakwater in Plymouth Sound (which took thirty-seven years to build and was completed by his son, also called John).

Rennie is probably best known for his bridge design, in particular the three in London: Waterloo Bridge, Southwark Bridge and London Bridge. Unfortunately, only London Bridge survives, but as a tourist attraction in the Arizona desert. After the opening of Waterloo Bridge, generally considered to be his masterpiece, he was offered a knighthood by the Prince Regent, but he declined it.

His two sons, George and John, worked with him on many of his projects, especially the three London bridges, and both had distinguished careers as engineers, including work on the early railways. After their father's death they took over the running of the manufacturing

Bust of John Rennie, overlooking what is left of his London Docks at Spirit Quay in Wapping.

business he had set up in Southwark, and it was there in 1835 that the second tunnelling shield was made for Marc Brunel's Thames Tunnel. The younger John is probably best known for supervising the construction of his father's London Bridge, after which he was offered a knighthood, which he accepted.

John Rennie senior was a strong and energetic man, nearly 6 feet 4 inches tall. He was a workaholic and was known to have taken only one holiday in his life, and that was a working holiday in France and the Netherlands, where he mostly spent his time visiting docks and other engineering projects. He took personal responsibility for all aspects of his business, designing everything himself without using assistants. According to his son, John, who wrote about him in his autobiography, he could be very quick-tempered, though he also knew how to control his temper, so that others thought him a very composed character.

He was buried in the crypt of St Paul's Cathedral, where his grave is marked by a modest slab of granite. He is also commemorated by a bust at Spice Quay, Wapping, overlooking what little remains of the London Docks he built.

When the medieval bridge was demolished, many Roman and medieval coins and other antiquities were discovered, and these are now in the British Museum. Two wooden medieval statues were also found in the river at that time, which had probably decorated the chapel. One, of a monk, is now in the British Museum; the other, of God the Father, is at Sudeley Castle in Gloucestershire. There was also a demand for souvenirs of the historic bridge, and the market was flooded with furniture and knick-knacks made with the wood from the starlings. Unfortunately, the remains of Peter de Colechurch, who had been buried in the crypt of the chapel, were not preserved but were most likely thrown into the Thames. A small casket in the Museum of London is said to contain some of his bones, but modern analysis has proved this to be untrue.

Much of the stonework was sold off, and it is still possible to see a few relics today. However, it must be borne in mind that almost all the surviving material is from the eighteenth-century reconstruction, not the original medieval bridge, despite a few claims to the contrary. One of the eighteenth-century alcoves can be seen in a quadrangle of Guy's Hospital, and two more are in Victoria Park, Hackney. A fourth one is in the gardens of a block of flats in East Sheen. Some of the balustrade was used on the seafront at Herne Bay, but this was lost in the great storm of 1953. One arch of the old bridge unexpectedly came to light on the north bank in 1921 when Adelaide House was rebuilt, but unfortunately its preservation was considered to be too expensive and it was destroyed, although one of the stones, from the eighteenth-century cladding, is now preserved in the churchyard of St Magnus the Martyr.

In 1863 pageantry returned to the bridge when it was sumptuously decorated to welcome Princess Alexandra of Denmark when she arrived to marry the Prince of Wales. Along both sides of the bridge, which was lined with members of the Honourable Artillery Company, were flags of both countries and portraits of Danish kings, and at the north end was a huge triumphal arch covered in allegorical figures.

In the early evening of Saturday 13 December 1884 an attempt was made to blow the bridge up. Although the bridge was full of pedestrians and road traffic, no one was killed and only a few were injured, and the bridge itself escaped serious damage, possibly because the device had been underwater when it went off. The explosion was heard as far away as Woolwich and Epping, and many windows were blown in on both sides of the river. The culprits were never caught, and they may have been killed in the explosion, but the general feeling was that the atrocity had been carried out by the Fenians, a group of Irish Republican extremists, who had already attempted to blow up a number of important buildings in London.

After the opening in 1836 of London Bridge station, the bridge had to contend with the extra crowds of City workers crossing it during the morning and evening rush hours. By the 1850s over a hundred thousand pedestrians used the bridge daily, and both the footpaths and the roadway were often extremely congested. The first suggestion that the bridge should be widened was put forward in 1854. The idea was to hang footpaths 12 feet wide over the sides of the bridge, though it would clearly not improve its architectural appearance. Similar proposals were made in 1869 and 1875, but they came to nothing, though it was clear that something had to be done. In 1882 plans were put forward for doubling the width of the bridge, but all

The Opening of
London Bridge in
*1831, a painting by
Clarkson Stanfield.*

such plans were put on hold when a new bridge at the Tower was proposed which, it was hoped, would ease the congestion.

More serious plans for the bridge's widening were discussed in 1900, when it was clear that, even after the construction of Tower Bridge, London Bridge was still unable to cope with the volume of traffic using it. The proposals met with much opposition, as it was felt by some that altering Rennie's bridge would severely damage the look of it, but work finally began in 1902. The operation involved cantilevering new footpaths out from the existing bridge, leaving room for a wider carriageway. The corbels and parapets were all of granite, to be in keeping with Rennie's structure. It was a complicated operation, as the bridge was kept open during the work, and temporary footbridges were put up on both sides. The new footpaths were declared fully open by the Lord Mayor in a ceremony at the end of March 1904. The work had cost £100,000 and was paid for by the Bridge House Estates.

By the 1960s Rennie's bridge could no longer cope with the demands placed on it. At first it was decided to widen the bridge again, but it was soon realised that it would have to be replaced by a more modern structure. The new bridge was designed by Harold Knox King, the City Engineer, with Lord Holford acting as architectural consultant, and Mott, Hay & Anderson as consulting engineers. The contractors were John Mowlem & Company, who tendered to build the bridge for just over £4 million. It is a three-arched cantilever bridge of pre-stressed concrete, clad in polished granite, and it is 100 feet wide, with a six-lane roadway. Work began in 1967 and lasted until 1972. There were complex problems to be solved in building the bridge, as it had to be on the same alignment as the old bridge, which had to be kept open during weekdays while the new bridge was being built. The solution was to build it in four sections, allowing pedestrians and traffic to use the rest of the bridge while each section was being constructed. The upstream quarter was built first, then the downstream section. The old bridge was then taken down so that the central sections could be constructed. Finally, all four sections were joined up and the surface added. All the work of construction and demolition was carried out using a massive gantry that rested on the piers of the old bridge. Each of the pre-cast units was hoisted into position and then suspended from the gantry until they could be joined up. The units are hollow, allowing essential services to cross the river – London Bridge is the only hollow bridge across the Thames. The downstream footpath was

London Bridge 1872 by Gustave Doré, showing massive congestion on the bridge and steamboats passing through it. The pier was the main departure point for the popular steamboat services.

Postcard showing London Bridge after it was widened in 1902.

made considerably wider than the upstream one, as this is the side most used by commuters arriving at London Bridge station, and the footpaths are heated in winter. The new bridge was opened by the Queen on 16 March 1973, when she unveiled a plaque on the downstream parapet to commemorate the event. The bridge had taken 4½ years to build and had cost £4.5 million, all of which came from the funds of the Bridge House Estates.

Soon after the plans for the new bridge were announced, the City started receiving letters from people wanting to buy parts of Rennie's bridge, so it was decided to offer the whole bridge for sale instead, as it was felt that it could serve a useful function somewhere else. Even before the prospectus was printed, there was interest from Universal Studios in Hollywood, but in the end the winning bid was from the McCullough Oil Company of the United States, who wanted to re-erect the bridge as the centrepiece of a new tourist attraction at Lake Havasu City in Arizona. They paid £1 million for the bridge and spent a further £100,000 in transporting it across the Atlantic. Over the next three years the facing stones were removed one by one and individually numbered before being shipped to America, where it was reconstructed. On 23 September 1968 the first stone was laid by the Lord Mayor of London, Sir Gilbert Inglefield, and three years later it was officially opened by the then Lord Mayor, Sir Peter Studd. A banquet was held, at which the menu enjoyed by William IV at the opening in 1831 was repeated. In a typical American touch, the master of ceremonies was television star Lorne Greene, from the series *Bonanza*. There is a much repeated urban myth that the Americans thought they were buying Tower Bridge, but this is complete nonsense, as the company had seen plans and drawings of the bridge before putting in a bid, and there is no way they could have confused the bridge they bought with one of the most recognisable bridges in the world.

In June 1984 a Royal Navy frigate, which had been moored alongside HMS *Belfast*, was attempting to turn round near London Bridge. Unfortunately, the captain misjudged the tide and hit the bridge, dislodging a few stones from the balustrade, and causing £25,000 worth of damage.

A few remnants of Rennie's bridge can still be seen, a few *in situ*. The most important are the abutment and arch at the southern end, which can be seen in Tooley Street. The stairs up to the bridge on the upstream side are known as Nancy's Steps, after a scene in Dickens' *Oliver Twist* in which Nancy is overheard giving information about Oliver, which leads to her death. Close by, outside the Mudlark public house, are several large blocks of granite from the old bridge, assembled to commemorate the Queen's Silver Jubilee in 1977, and, at the southern end of the bridge itself, there are two more blocks on the pavement. More unexpectedly, four granite slabs from the bridge can be seen beside the lake in Kew Gardens, where they were once used as a feeding platform for waterfowl. On either side of the northern end of the bridge you can still see the ashlar outer walls of the river steps of the old bridge. Under the first arch on the north side of the bridge, on the parapet alongside the Thames Path, are four lamp standards carrying the emblems of the City of London and the Bridge House Estates. The original bridge had three-branched lamps, but after the bridge's widening the lamps were single ones, much like these, so it is possible that they also come from Rennie's bridge.

One of the ancient privileges of receiving the Freedom of the City, or so tradition has it, is to be able to herd sheep across London Bridge, though there is no documentary evidence of the right. Freemen used to be exempt from paying tolls, and livestock was once regularly herded through the streets on the way to market, often across the bridges, so this could have included the right to drive a herd of sheep over London Bridge without paying for the privilege. In the popular consciousness, this privilege has been considered, incorrectly, to be a right bestowed on Freemen today, though it is a privilege rarely carried out, except occasionally as a publicity stunt.

Every July the bridge forms the backdrop for the start of the Doggett's Coat and Badge Race, the oldest contested race in the sporting calendar. It was initiated in 1715 by Thomas Doggett to celebrate the accession of George I, and he left money in his will to the Fishmongers' Company to pay for the coat and badge to be presented to the winning young waterman. The race is still rowed over the original course, from London Bridge to Chelsea, and usually takes about thirty minutes.

There are a number of things to look out for on the modern bridge. On both sides of the road on the south side are silver dragons marking the boundary between the City of London and the London Borough of Southwark. On the downstream parapet near the centre of the bridge is the plaque marking the opening of the bridge in 1973. On the centre of both balustrades are Silver Jubilee Walkway plaques identifying all the buildings of interest visible from the bridge. On the upstream side at foot level can be seen the boundary marks of the parishes of St Magnus the Martyr and St Saviour's (now Southwark Cathedral), preserved from the old bridge.

In February 2008 a new attraction opened up in the vaults under the southern abutment of Rennie's bridge. The London Bridge Experience has created scenes from

Modern London Bridge.

the gorier side of the life of the bridge using actors to bring them to life. Though this gives only a very limited idea of the bridge's history, there is a small museum at the end of a visit, which contains items from the collection of the late Peter Jackson, a historian fascinated by the bridge.

Today London Bridge is still busy at all times of day, but in particular during the morning and evening rush hours, when hundreds of thousands of commuters cross it to and from London Bridge Station. The scene is described in T. S. Eliot's celebrated 1922 poem *The Waste Land*, lines that have a curious aptness, as the poet worked for eight years in a bank:

> Unreal City,
> Under the brown fog of a winter dawn,
> A crowd flowed over London Bridge, so many,
> I had not thought death had undone so many.

TOWER BRIDGE

TOWER BRIDGE is one of London's best-known landmarks and, with its unique design, is instantly recognised throughout the world. With its mock-medieval look, many visitors are fooled into thinking it is much older than it is, but inside its Gothic granite exterior is a steel frame, which is a masterpiece of Victorian engineering.

For much of the nineteenth century there had been discussions about the need for new river crossings downstream of London Bridge, partly to take pressure off London Bridge, which was becoming very congested, but also to cater for the needs of a growing population to the east of the City, whose only means of crossing the river was by ferry or a very long detour. Although it was generally agreed that a new bridge was needed, there was still opposition from vested interests, mainly from those who feared that access for ships would be impeded and trade would suffer. Various committees discussed the project and negotiations continued for many years over such matters as whether it should be a high-level or low-level bridge, how it would be financed and, even as late as 1878, whether it should be a toll bridge or not. The last question was almost redundant, as plans were already in hand to free the rest of London's bridges from toll. Those working in the dock and wharf trades, however, continued to be opposed to a bridge, as they felt it would affect their livelihood; they

Detail of an 1862 proposal from Peter William Barlow and Robert Richardson for a suspension bridge on the site of Tower Bridge. Somewhat incongruously, the approaches are based on the Leaning Tower of Pisa.

preferred a tunnel, which would not interfere with the operations of the Port of London.

The problem was that the bridge would have to allow tall ships into the busy Upper Pool, and finding a solution was no easy matter. A low-level bridge would interfere with the river traffic, but a high-level bridge would need steep approaches, which would be difficult for vehicles. The earliest proposal, put forward in 1824 by Samuel Brown, was for a suspension bridge, but nothing happened for another fifty years. When the scheme was seriously discussed in the 1870s, many weird and wonderful plans were put forward. One was for a raised platform running on rails in the riverbed; another involved taking carriages up in hydraulic lifts to cross by a high-level bridge; the most interesting one was a low-level 'duplex' bridge that split into two carriageways in the middle, each with a swing-bridge, so traffic could switch from one to the other when ships needed to pass through it. Others proposed a tunnel or ferry, and in 1878 Sir Joseph Bazalgette put forward several designs for a high-level bridge, as well as proposals for tunnels at Rotherhithe and Blackwall, and a free ferry at Woolwich. His bridge designs were rejected as they did not allow enough headroom, and only the Woolwich ferry was in operation during his lifetime.

One of the biggest problems was raising the funds to build the three crossings, and in 1883 Parliament turned down a petition by the Metropolitan Board of Works for the extension of coal and wine duties to finance them, with the extraordinary reason that 'it had not yet been shown that they were required'. In the end, although the bridge is outside the City limits, it was agreed that the City's Bridge House Estates would fund the new bridge.

At one point it seemed likely that a low-level swing-bridge would be built, but in the end the most acceptable design came from the City Architect, Horace Jones: a bascule bridge that could open like a double drawbridge to allow ships through. In the original design there was a curved arch over the centre of the bridge, and the bascules would be opened by chains. The design was amended, as the roadway could

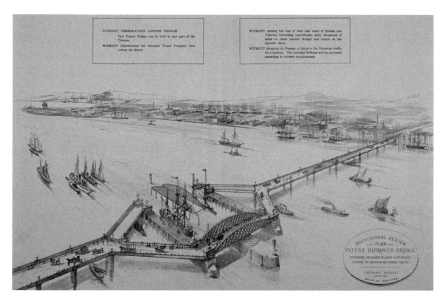

Frederic Barnett's 1876 design for a duplex low-level Tower Bridge, which he claimed would allow an uninterrupted flow of traffic both along and over the river.

not be opened far enough to allow ships through, and hydraulic power was introduced instead to raise the bascules. Jones worked up the designs with the engineer John Wolfe Barry for presentation to Parliament, and in 1885 the Tower Bridge Bill received the Royal Assent. The resulting bridge is a combination of three different types: suspension bridges at each end, a girder bridge for the pedestrian walkways, and a bascule bridge in the centre. The City asked Jones, who was knighted in 1886, to share the supervision of the construction with Barry, but in 1887 Jones died suddenly, and Barry took on the direction of the whole operation, helped by, among others, Henry Marc Brunel, son of Isambard. The cost of construction was originally estimated to be £750,000, but the final cost was over £1 million, including the cost of the approaches. The Corporation had been given four years to complete the construction, but it had to ask for two extensions and it was eight years before the job was completed. Part of the problem was that it was a legal requirement to keep the river clear at all times for ships to go through, which meant that the two piers could not be built at the same time. Considering the size and complexity of the task, it was a considerable achievement that only ten men died during the bridge's construction.

On 21 June 1886 the first stone was laid on the northern abutment by the Prince of Wales on behalf of the Queen, with considerable ceremony. As is traditional on such occasions, a time capsule containing coins and newspapers of the time was placed underneath it. The stone can still be seen on the upstream side of the northern abutment, alongside the wharf.

The foundations of the piers were dug out inside wrought-iron caissons sunk 25 feet into the riverbed and filled with concrete. The piers, 70 feet wide and 185 feet long, were built with Staffordshire bricks with granite facings. They were built hollow, as they had to contain massive chambers for the counterbalanced ends of the bascules. The towers were built with a skeleton of steel girders, making them strong enough to take the strain of opening the central bascules, and were additionally braced by three landing floors and the iron walkways. The walkways consist of two 95-foot cantilevers, which support a central linking girder. The side spans are supported by steel suspension chains attached to the main towers and the abutment towers. All the steelwork was supplied and built by Sir William Arrol & Company. It was made in Glasgow and delivered by steamers to be assembled on site, using cranes, which were moved up as each stage was completed. Great care was taken at all times to prevent any tools or rivets falling into the river, as many boats, including pleasure steamers, were constantly passing through. So as not to obstruct the passage of ships, the bascules had to be built in the vertical position.

Hydraulic machinery was installed in the piers to operate the bascules, as well as the lifts that would take pedestrians up to the walkways when the bridge was open, though staircases were also provided. To save on power, each of the bascules is loaded at its lower end with 130 tons of pig iron and lead, and the total weight of each bascule is 1,200 tons. All the hydraulic machinery was supplied by Sir William Armstrong, Mitchell & Company, and the steam engines to drive it were placed on the south side of the bridge, under the approach road. All of the machinery was installed in duplicate, as an insurance against anything going wrong. When the bridge first opened, it took two minutes to raise the bascules. The hydraulics were replaced by electricity in 1976, though much of the old machinery was preserved and can still be seen.

The towers are covered in Cornish granite, with Portland stone dressings, none of it stress-bearing, rather like the cladding on modern steel-framed buildings. The bridge has a medieval look, as it was specified that it had to be in keeping with the nearby Tower of London. Horace Jones' original plan was for the bridge to be clad in red brick, but Barry's architectural assistant, George D. Stevenson, made a number of changes to the architectural detailing. He added windows, balconies and other features to add visual interest, and the result is more like a Scottish castle than an English one.

The length of the bridge is 940 feet and the central span is 200 feet. The central roadway is 50 feet wide, with the side spans being 60 feet wide. The gradients are much less steep than on most other bridges, and on the north side it is almost level, which was of great benefit to hauliers with heavy loads, and certainly kinder to the horses.

Engraving from the Illustrated London News *of the work to construct the piers of Tower Bridge.*

Work on the bridge was completed in 1894. On 27 March the two bascules were lowered for the first time, marking the bridge's completion, and they were later tested by having a huge weight placed on the southern one, including traction engines and carts loaded with granite. The bridge was officially opened on Saturday 30 June by the Prince of Wales, who had laid the foundation stone eight years earlier. The opening was a day of great pageantry, with the streets full of people and the Thames full of boats, all helped by the glorious weather. The royal procession, accompanied by an escort of Life Guards, drove from Marlborough House to the Mansion House, where it was met by the Lord Mayor, before continuing to the bridge. The Prince and Princess, accompanied by other members of the royal family, marked the opening of the bridge to land traffic by processing in their carriages across it and back again to a pavilion full of special guests. The Prince then opened the bridge to river traffic by operating a lever with the lid of a loving cup, which was set on a pedestal (the cup, engraved with an image of the bridge, was later presented to him). As the bascules rose there was a fanfare of trumpets, a gun salute from the Tower and a cacophony of steamboat whistles. Twelve decorated steamboats then passed through the bridge, one of them carrying a band playing the National Anthem. The royal party returned to Westminster by steamboat, passing between rows of gaily decorated boats. The colourful scene was captured for posterity in a painting by William Lionel Wylie, now on show at the Guildhall Art Gallery. After the successful event, the Lord Mayor received a baronetcy, but Barry was only made a Companion of the Bath for his efforts; he had to wait until 1897 for his knighthood.

The great enterprise was considered to be a huge success. In the words of the French writer Alphonse Daudet, 'It is the most colossal symbol of what human effort can accomplish'. Whilst generally considered to be a great engineering triumph, not everyone felt it was a great piece of architecture. The architectural treatment of the

The Opening of Tower Bridge on 30 June 1894 *by William Lionel Wylie.*

bridge was much criticised in some quarters, with some saying it was a sham and that its steel skeleton should have been left as it was, like the Forth Railway Bridge, though others suggested that the naked steel framework would have looked ugly in such a prominent location. One would have thought that the adverse views would have mellowed with familiarity, but not so. In 1909 *The Times* was particularly scathing, saying that 'it looks like a monstrous Gothic toy that ought to be one of the side-shows of an exhibition', and George Bernard Shaw commented in 1924 that 'engineering bridges are offensive only when they are artistically pretentious, like the Tower Bridge'. As late as 1952 Nikolaus Pevsner, the architectural historian, referred to the 'barren Gothic towers' and says of the bridge that 'The massive structure does much damage to the skyline of the City'. To the general public, however, it has always been a great favourite and has become one of London's most enduring icons, its unique profile appearing on postcards and souvenirs bought in great numbers by visitors to the city.

Not everyone welcomed the royal opening of the bridge. A number of anarchists were arrested for inciting others to murder any members of the royal family who attended the opening. The day before the big day, they were on Tower Hill, carrying placards with sentiments such as: 'Fellow workers, you have expended Life Energy and Skill in Building this Bridge … now come the Royal Vermin and Rascally Politicians with Pomp and Ceremony to claim all the credi …' Others enjoyed the new bridge rather too much, and after the opening there was a spate of incidents in which people jumped off the bridge, either for a wager or simply for the hell of it. One well-planned stunt went seriously wrong in November. Benjamin Fuller, a professional diver who claimed to have jumped from all the other bridges in London, disguised himself with a wig and false moustache and managed to get through a trapdoor on to the roof of one of the walkways. From there he dived into the Thames but drowned because of the strong tide.

The bridge was opened to pedestrians on the Monday, when 141,000 people took the opportunity to inspect it at close quarters, and the following weekend the numbers were even greater. Vehicles were first allowed on to the bridge two days later, and within a month the bridge was carrying a third as many vehicles as had been using London Bridge before the new bridge was opened, giving users of the older bridge at least some temporary relief. During its first year, up to eight thousand vehicles and sixty thousand pedestrians crossed the bridge daily.

Building the new approaches involved a considerable amount of demolition, and bodies had to be exhumed from a burial ground in the Tower to make way for the northern approaches, which were ready on time. On the south side the Corporation built the new roadway as far as Tooley Street, but the construction of a new link to the New and Old Kent Roads was the responsibility of the London County Council, which had taken on the duties of the MBW in 1889. Unfortunately, work on this section of the approaches had not even been begun by the time the bridge opened, so that southbound traffic still had to negotiate a maze of narrow, winding streets. The delay was caused by the LCC's attempt to get Parliament to agree to a 'betterment' scheme, in which property owners would be charged for the increased value to their property after the improvements.

The City was legally required to provide a tug to help ships navigate the bridge during and after its construction. In early 1896 it proposed discontinuing the service, but, after much opposition, the proposal was dropped, and the tug continued to operate until after the Second World War. Stables were also provided, so that horses would be on hand to help horse-drawn vehicles across the bridge and so alleviate congestion. This service operated until the 1930s. In the days before the advent of the internal combustion engine, every time the bridge was opened horse droppings would roll down the slope of the rising road, and two men, armed with shovels, were employed to keep it clear by disposing of the droppings through the small doors which can still be seen on the outer walls of the towers.

When it opened, the bridge required a staff of eighty to operate it, including the Bridgemaster, his deputy, a Resident Engineer, fifty-seven men to operate the machinery, eight constables and a maintenance team of carpenters, plumbers and blacksmiths. The Bridgemaster and Engineer originally lived in flats in the abutment towers (there is still a sign on the southern abutment that reads 'Bridgemaster's Dining Room'). Today the bridge still needs thirteen people to maintain it, and about sixty people work on the bridge in various capacities.

The interests of shipping meant that the bridge originally had to stay open for two hours at high tide, which was why the upper walkways were provided for pedestrians to cross when the bridge was open, but this rule was soon relaxed and the walkways were not used as much as the authorities had expected. Most people preferred to wait at ground level and watch the bridge opening, rather than walk up or wait for a lift to take them up, with another walk or wait to get down, all of which would probably have taken longer than the average wait for the bridge to reopen. The walkways were no doubt a good place for a stroll, but in 1910 they were closed through lack of use. It has been suggested the closure was due to the number of suicides, but this cannot have been true, as the walkways were enclosed by cast-iron latticework, making it impossible to jump from there, though there were a number of suicides from the roadway.

Originally the bridge opened up to twenty times a day, and it opened 6,160 times in its first full year. These days, although the Upper Pool is no longer a working dock area, it still opens about a thousand times a year. The maximum lift is 87 degrees, though it rises above 35 degrees only when necessary, in order to save time. Originally there was no need for a ship to warn of its arrival; two black balls hanging from the mast were an indication of its intention to pass through the bridge. There was a system of semaphore by day and lights at night to inform shipping of the position of the bascules. Even today, shipping takes precedence over road traffic, and any vessel can ask for it to be opened so long as twenty-four hours notice is given. This can cause unexpected delays, and no one is exempt, as President Clinton discovered in 1996 when, after a meal at the Pont de la Tour with Tony Blair, his motorcade was held up while the bridge opened, much to the consternation of his security staff.

In 1912 Frank McLean, piloting a small biplane, became the first man to fly through Tower Bridge, then flying under all the other bridges as far as Westminster. On the return journey he tried to repeat the feat, but at Tower Bridge turbulence caused the plane to crash into the Thames. The feat has often been repeated, most

A Swedish sailing ship passing through Tower Bridge.

famously in 1968, by an RAF fighter pilot flying at up to 300 mph. A year later a light aircraft flew through the bridge on Battle of Britain Sunday as a tribute to those pilots who lost their lives during the war.

The bridge was not seriously damaged during the Second World War, though windows and tiles were broken and some of the stone cladding was dislodged or loosened by the air attacks. The bridge had its own anti-aircraft battery, and the control cabins were plated in steel and sandbagged as a precaution. On one occasion the bridge had a narrow escape when a doodlebug went through the middle of it, though the tug took a direct hit and the two staff on board were killed. In 1943 W. F. C. Holden, the architect of the National Provincial Bank, put forward a proposal that, instead of repairing any war damage to the bridge, it should be encased in glass and re-used as offices after the war!

The most famous incident on the bridge occurred in 1952, when the bascules began to open before a number 78 bus had managed to cross. The bus dropped about 3 feet from the north bascule, which had started rising too soon, on to the south bascule, injuring ten people, including the driver. The City Corporation accepted responsibility for the error, and the driver was awarded £10 by London Transport.

During its history, Tower Bridge has rarely failed to operate. One occasion was during the heatwave of 1968, when it was unable to close properly as metal locks had expanded in the heat. Firemen had to spray the locks with water and the bridge was temporarily closed to traffic. More embarrassingly, in 2005 the bridge jammed in the upright position after letting a ship through, because of a computer failure, which took ten hours to correct, causing serious traffic problems.

The bridge has occasionally been hit by ships, and one of the most dramatic incidents occurred in 2004, when a three-masted training ship tried to sail through, its master believing that it had been arranged for the bridge to open, which was not the case. The pilot attempted to contact the bridge, but when he realised the bridge

INDEX

Page numbers in italic refer to illustrations

FURTHER READING

Cookson, Brian. *Crossing the River*. Mainstream Publishing, 2006.

Croad, Stephen. *London's Bridges*. Her Majesty's Stationery Office, 1983.

Home, Gordon. *Old London Bridge*. The Bodley Head, 1931.

Jackson, Peter. *London Bridge: a Visual History*. Historical Publications, 1971 and 2002.

McFetrich, David. *Spanning the River – Artists' Views of Thames Bridges*. Guildhall Art Gallery, 2006.

Phillips, Geoffrey. *Thames Crossings*. David & Charles, 1981.

Pierce, Patricia. *Old London Bridge*. Headline, 2001.

Pudney, John. *Crossing London's River*. J. M. Dent, 1972.

Roberts, Chris. *Cross River Traffic*. Granta, 2005.

Sudjic, Deyan. *Blade of Light – The Story of London's Millennium Bridge*. Penguin, 2001.

Walker, R. J. B. *Old Westminster Bridge – The Bridge of Fools*. David & Charles, 1979.

Ward, Robert. *The Man Who Buried Nelson – the Surprising Life of Robert Mylne*. Tempus, 2007.

Watson, Bruce. *Old London Bridge – Lost and Found*. Museum of London Archaeological Service, 2004.

Watson, Bruce; Bingham, Trevor; and Dyson, Tony. *London Bridge: 2,000 Years of a River Crossing*. Museum of London Archaeological Service, 2001.

Aerial view from 1932 of the present Hampton Court Bridge nearing completion alongside the nineteenth-century iron bridge. The square spaces where Lutyens planned to build pavilions are clearly visible.

was not going to open, he tried to turn the ship around, hitting the south pier, and it had to be pulled clear by a tug. Fortunately no one on the ship was injured and no serious damage was caused to the bridge.

The hydraulics were replaced by electricity in 1976, but when the change happened it was decided to keep two pumping engines and four of the engines driving the bascules *in situ*. What was surplus to requirements was sold off. As with the original equipment, the new electrical units supply twice as much power as is strictly necessary. Now only one person is needed to operate the machinery, and it needs far less maintenance, which makes the bridge more economical to run. This also meant that it was now possible to consider opening the bridge as a tourist attraction. The bridge had originally been painted chocolate brown, Queen Victoria's favourite colour, and later a dull grey, but in 1976 it was repainted in blue and white, with touches of red and gold. The whole bridge was refurbished, which included replacing damaged stonework and repairing or replacing damaged windows. Much of the cast-iron decoration that had been taken down during the Second World War was also replaced, but made now of lighter glass-reinforced plastic. This included the giant City coat of arms and the smaller emblems of the Bridge House Estates, which now adorn the upper walkways. New lifts were installed to replace the old hydraulic ones, and the walkways were glassed in. On 30 June 1982, eighty-eight years after it first opened, the bridge was reopened to the public as a museum, named the Tower Bridge Exhibition. Visitors can enjoy the views from the walkways, see the engine rooms and learn about the history of the bridge. To find out more, including when the bridge opens to let ships through, visit the website www.towerbridge.org.uk During the winter, they offer more specialist behind-the-scenes tours, which take in places that cannot normally be visited, including the engines that operate the bascules and the enormous bascule chambers, which alone are worth the visit. These need to be booked in advance.

On the northern approach there is a curiosity noticed by few people. The Tower had agreed to give up part of the Tower Ditch for the bridge approaches, and they were allowed to occupy some of the arches under the approach road. One of them houses a uniform store and a guardroom, and its location is marked by a single cast-iron chimney among the line of cast-iron lamp standards standing on the balustrade.

Being such an important London landmark, Tower Bridge regularly appears in films, but usually as an establishing shot. One film that did rather more than that was the John Wayne film *Brannigan*, which, imitating the bus incident mentioned above, staged a spectacular chase in which a car jumps over the half-opened bridge.

An early morning view of Tower Bridge and the Pool of London.